Wade Fishing the

North Branch of the Potomac

Including the Casselman, Savage, Youghiogheny and Trout Streams

By Steve Moore

Steve Moore is an avid fisherman. He was ruined for life when his father introduced him to the sport at the age of 8 while the family lived in Norway as a result of military duty. Chasing trout on mountain streams left an enduring imprint and drive to find new water... something that tortures Steve to this day.

Of course, this was preordained since Steve's father was fishing in a local bass tournament on the morning he was born. His father claims to have had permission to go, but Steve's mother does not remember the actual facts matching that story. The point that he won a nice Shakespeare reel did nothing to mitigate the trouble he was in upon his return.

Published by Calibrated Consulting, Inc
ISBN: 978-0-9861003-3-8
Feedback: feedback@catchguide.com

Dedication

I would like to dedicate this book to several important people in my life:

- My wife, Donna, who has put up with my fishing addiction for 40 years. Thankfully, she is an avid bass angler whose gentle touch hauls in more of the big boys than I do.
- My father, Hal Moore, who patiently taught all of his children how to fish at an early age
- My fishing buddy, Dick Sherwood, who convinced me to switch from spin to fly fishing and opened an exciting new door. Various fishing equipment vendors are grateful to him as I fell victim to the "new guy" syndrome of buying too much "stuff"

Other Book books by Steve Moore:

Wade Fishing the Rappahannock River of Virginia
Smallmouth Bass and Shad

Wade Fishing the Rapidan River of Virginia
From Smallmouth Bass to Trout

Wade and Shoreline Fishing the Potomac River for Smallmouth Bass
Chain Bridge to Harpers Ferry

Maryland Trout Fishing
The Stocked and Wild Rivers, Streams, Lakes and Ponds

Table of Contents

Introduction 1

General Perspective 2

Flies and Lures to Use 4

Water Volume / Flow 6

Best Time to Fish 11

Understanding the Rating System 14

Piedmont/Westernport 18

Bloomington 24

Barnum North C&R 32

Barnum Put and Take 37

Barnum South C&R 43

Paul Sarbanes Trail 49

Jennings Randolph Lake 53

Kitzmiller 58

Lostland Run 70

Laurel Run 80

Wallman 84

Stony River 98

Gormania 102

Bayard 107

Garrett County Trout Streams 112

Casselman River 125

Savage River 128

Youghiogheny River 134

Gage Height 145

Water Temperature 147

Introduction

I want to provide a different sort of guide.

I want to share a detailed, focused guide to the North Branch. Beyond setting the stage, I will not talk about the North Branch in general terms because every mile offers a different fishing experience. As we walk up the river, I will show you the specific areas I fished and discuss what I encountered. I'll tell you how to get there, where to park, how to get to the stream, and what to use in the spots I found most productive.

This edition expands the coverage beyond the North Branch, although not at the same level of detail, to include the access points and information on other key Garrett county fishing spots drawn from my Maryland Trout Fishing Book. Use it to get to the Savage, Casselman and Youghiogheny rivers as well as the best wild and stocked trout water in the county. Inclusion of that additional material makes this a more comprehensive reference for Garrett County.

Given that a picture is worth a 1,000 words, I'll provide many of them – and I hope that you find the pictures to be the most informative aspect of the book. I don't know about you, but I have spent hours driving to places that proved to be a disappointment. If I had had the opportunity to look at the water first via pictures, I would have gone someplace else.

The section of the North Branch of the Potomac I cover in this guide is all public water. As such, there are no secrets. The fact that the vibrant trout fishery in North Branch exists is fully disclosed in the Maryland State stocking table that includes Google™ map links to the stocked areas as well as on the West Virginia fisheries mapping application and stocking plan. A quick click and you have a bird's eye view from the satellite picture.

I want to enhance your fishing experience with the precise information I include in this guide. The better time each of us has fishing, the more likely it is that we will purchase licenses year after year and introduce our friends and children to the quiet sport. In these difficult economic times, it is critical to ensure outdoor programs are fully funded as license sales provide a significant input to each state's outdoor recreation budget. Those trout stamps we purchase support the hatchery programs that produce the stocked trout that drive our passion every spring and fall.

It goes without saying that all of us must follow the fishing regulations. Please do not harvest trout in catch and release areas or during the delayed harvest season. That just ruins the experience for all and even hurts you the next time you go to that same spot to fish. On the other hand, I encourage people to keep fish in those stretches of the river that will not support trout once the water heats up in the summer.

Steve Moore

General Perspective

The fishable part of the North Branch spans approximately 30 miles of which 13 miles is controlled by special regulations including both delayed harvest and catch and return sections. Of the total, 21 miles are above the Jennings-Randolph dam and 9 are below. Having walked many miles along the river, I can assure you it would take years of focused effort to fish every nook and cranny of this spectacular river - even I look forward to many more years of discovery to add to my experience and perspective.

The stocked section of the North Branch begins at the northern end of the town of Westernport where the river borders 1st Street and ends miles south (upstream) at the bridge in the small town of Wilson. While the content and character of the river changes - moving from narrow to wide, fast to slow, deep to shallow - the one thing consistent is it runs most of its course in a breathtaking, narrow valley full of trees protected by steep hills. The hills bordering the river create an exciting, exceptionally beautiful setting for a great day of fishing whether you catch anything or not. In a general sense, if you were to fly at low level from Westernport to Wilson, you would see the river change from being broad and slow in the northern reaches to tight and fast once into the delayed harvest area in the Potomac State Forest above Kitzmiller. The highlight of your day might just be sitting on a flat rock in the middle of the stream sucking down a hot cup of coffee while you let the sun warm your face and enjoy the spectacular view.

In the Barnum section south of Westernport, the river is a cold water, year-round fishery that supports an active population of cutthroat, brown and stocked rainbow trout. It ends at the Jennings-Randolph Dam and the disposition of both the river and fishing change dramatically. The lake formed by the dam supports trout, bass and walleye; cradling them in the unusually deep sections formed by the surrounding steep hills.

Above the dam, the river reverts to natural temperature and flow characteristics that align your pursuit for trout to the stocking programs of Maryland and West Virginia. Your only hope for cool water in the summer rests with the feeder streams spilling their water into the North Branch. Each of these becomes a potential target for your fishing day as many of them attract trout as the water warms. In addition, there is one formally designated river, the Stony River, that pushes into the North Branch from the south in the Wallman section. It is the reason for the significant difference in water volume measured at the Steyer and Kitzmiller gages.

Above the lake, the amount of water diminishes the farther upstream you go; becoming a trickle at Wilson. By August in dry hot years, the trout are either caught or dead as a result of water temperatures that can spike up to 80°. However, the smallmouth bass shrug off the heat better than their finny cousins and cruise the deep, cooler pools; lonely and rejected when the trout hunters leave. You don't need a four-wheel drive vehicle to point your rod into the vast majority of the water of the North Branch. Where I recommend a high clearance vehicle, I note it. In addition, there are plenty of areas where you do not need to break brush, shoot an azimuth through the woods, or take exceptional measures to find good water. In fact, in the "Put and Take" section below Barnum, the river runs right next the road for several miles; making it an ideal stretch for those who may not be as young and robust as we all wish we still were.

The remoteness of the North Branch might make you leap to the conclusion that it is not fully supported by an active, aggressive stocking program. Thankfully, both Maryland and West Virginia stock this water, so it sees more than its fair share in a given year. Maryland stocks the remote areas from a tank truck outfitted to ride the rails via a cooperative agreement with the CSX Company. In early 2015, Maryland deposited 14,900 trout into the North Branch with West Virginia adding thousands more to the mix. In many years, one or the other State will stock large brood trout as late as August to add to the excitement of this water.

Be prepared before you get to the trailhead. There are not many facilities once you move upstream from Westernport. The gas station in Kitzmiller burned down years ago leaving only the Coal Bucket Cafe, on West Main Street near the bridge. Granted, you can detour over to Oakland for gas, but that's a long drive that will keep you off the water for at least 90 minutes -- so be sure you have all your supplies before you hit the water.

When you talk to fishermen who spend time on the North Branch, the one thing they will all agree and comment on is that the rocks are shaped with the perfect dimensions to twist your ankle as you dance your way upstream trying to balance on their snot-slick surfaces. The North Branch has its own brand of sadistic slime coating everything as a result of the addition of lime to offset the impact of the acid water resulting from old, environmentally unconscious mining operations. There is no sure footing anywhere you go on this river. *If you fish here without a wading staff, you are a fool who will not be long for this world*.

The Maryland Department of Natural Resources has done a good job of carving the river into different regulatory areas. There's something here for everybody whether you are a catch and return purist or need to take a few fish home with you for dinner. The "Put and Take" sections alternate with the special regulation areas; allowing fishermen to experience the full variety of this river regardless of the type of fishing they pursue. Depending on where you fish, you can use bait. There are restrictions on keeping fish based on calendar date in some sections. Finally, you must be aware of the river conditions. The quality of the fishing depends on the amount and the temperature of the water. Fortunately, the US Geological Survey sponsors a diverse set of gages on the North Branch that provide real-time statistics on what is happening. In the chapter on gages, I provide the historical information you need to plan trips. Never, ever take the long drive to the North Branch without checking the gages! The DNR does not have the capability to validate access along every inch of the stocked water in the state and you must be alert for any "No Trespassing" or "Posted" signs a landowner might erect. Finally, do not walk on train tracks since it is automatically considered to be posted in both Maryland and West Virginia. It is my understanding that crossing the tracks to move from parking to river is still permitted.

Important Note: I show GPS coordinates using a format compatible with Google™ Maps. Google tends to jump to a landmark shown with a RED arrow. Look for the GREEN arrow. The only difference between Google and what you would use in your handheld GPS is a "negative" sign in front of the second coordinate. To program these into your GPS, remove the negative and everything should work fine. For example, the Wallman Middle parking area is at GPS 39.315059,-79.284339. When you put this into your GPS, enter 39.315059, 79.284339.

Flies and Lures to Use

Fly Fishing

There is one small bit of history you need to understand to be successful on this river. Twenty years ago, it was dead water as a result of acid leaching from mines. The key thing you need to know is that "dead" meant dead to **ALL** life. There were no insect hatches possible in the acid water. Through the vision of Bob Bachman of the Maryland Department of Natural Resources, the river was transformed by the addition of lime dosers to neutralize the acid. If curious, you can see one on the right as you drive into Lostland Run. The Maryland DNR introduced smallmouth bass into the river 1993 followed by trout in 1994. As of 2015, both species are thriving where the water temperature matches their normal range. Over time, this is slowly correcting itself as the river becomes fertile enough to support the embedded insect activity that drives most fly fishing tactics. People who fish the river are starting to report good hatch activity, but it is not at the volume or consistency you would expect on an established trout stream.

Given that, your first fly choice should be a streamer pattern that mimics baitfish. If you see indications of insect presence, grab a bug and switch to something that is a close match. Here is a generic hatch chart derived from many sources and includes my opinions and observations. Until the insect population becomes fully entrenched and stable, this can only be a general guide.

Hatch Chart	Jan	Feb	Mar	Apr	May	Jun	Jul	Aug	Sep	Oct	Nov	Dec	Size
Black Stonefly		■	■										16 - 20
Brown Stonefly			■										14
Blue Quill				■									16 - 18
Blue Wing Olive				■	■	■			■	■			14 - 16
Red Quill					■	■	■	■					14 - 16
Quill Gordon				■	■								12 - 14
Cream Caddis					■	■	■	■	■	■	■		12 - 14
Hendrickson				■									10
Sulpher				■	■	■	■						14 - 18
March Brown				■	■	■							10 - 14
Green Caddis					■	■							14 - 16
Cream Variant					■	■							12 - 14
Light Cahill					■	■	■	■					12 - 14
Cricket							■	■	■				8 - 12
Hopper							■	■	■				8 - 12
Flying Ant							■	■	■				14 - 18
Beetles						■	■	■	■	■			14 - 16
Cranefly								■	■	■			12 - 14
Midge									■	■			20 - 22

Confused? Just make sure your fly box has a supply of the following in various sizes and match them to the bug you see on the water:

- Adams, Elk Hair Caddis, Blue Wing Olives
- Wulffs and Humpy
- Stoneflies
- Streamers – black, brown, white or yellow buggers, clousers, crawfish
- Nymphs – pheasant tail, copper john, hare's ear
- Green weenie, San Juan worms
- Other attractor patterns and terrestrials (hoppers, ants, etc)

Spin Fishing

Well, you can't go wrong with the following "hatch" chart:

Weather	Spinner Color
Cloudy	Silver
Sunny	Gold
Either	Small Rapalas

In addition to spinners (Panther Martin, Mepps, etc.), you should bring rapala trout pattern plugs with you. When spin fishing, I prefer the jointed version that is four inches long. The floating versions can be great for the smallmouth on the upper North Branch as the rapalas can double as top water plugs. Throw them out and twitch to trigger some explosive top water activity!

Use 1/8 or 1/4 oz. spinners. There may be rare occasions when you will want to go heavier or lighter. Body color is your choice. I always have good luck with silver spinner/yellow body or gold spinner/black body.

Water Volume / Flow

Knowledge of the current river conditions will save you a significant amount of frustration and heartache. The quality of the fishing comes and goes with the amount and the temperature of the water. If you are aware of what to expect and know where to check to determine the current conditions, you will avoid wasted treks out to the hinterland of Western Maryland only to discover an unfishable situation. This chapter looks at the USGS gages that apply to the various sections of the North Branch and provides guidance on how to interpret them.

As a general statement, to be fishable, the water flow (measured in cubic feet per second – "cfs" or gage height in feet) must be below the minimum level to make whitewater addicts happy. There is a great website – www.americanwhitewater.org – those folks use to determine put-in and take-out points and share conditions. The website has real-time river flow status (the site shows colors (red-yellow-green)) as shown below:

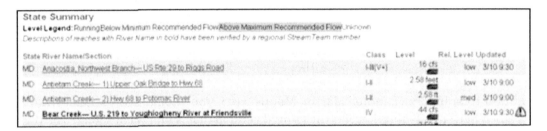

When you click on the section of the river you are interested in, it provides the guidance on minimum whitewater levels as you can see from this extract on the Barnum section:

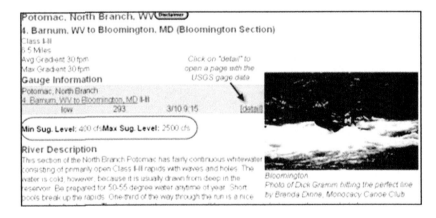

It is important to point out that the minimum whitewater level may still be above the maximum fishing level, so be careful. One item to note is that if you fish the river below the minimum level, you will probably not have kayakers floating over the great hole you just started to work.

Barnum Downstream through Piedmont/Westernport

The Barnum gage covers the section below the dam.

There are special whitewater releases you should be aware of and watch for. In addition to special releases, the Army Corps of Engineers provides a high volume release twice in April and May for the whitewater crowd. The river will not be fishable when those are underway. Check this page (http://www.nab-wc.usace.army.mil/northBranch.html) for the details on scheduled releases.

The Mineral County Parks and Recreation Commission Spring sponsors the whitewater releases and you can reach them at (304) 788-5732 for further information. For all other release information, call the operations center of the dam at (410) 962-7687.

Understanding the volume of water in the river is critical to both your safety and opportunity to catch fish. Most of the experts recommend you stay away from the river at levels above 550 to 600 cfs. In general, the quality of the fishing experience declines rapidly between 400 and 550 cfs. On the other end of the spectrum, the river is considered low when it is at 200 cfs or below. Here is a table that shows the average cfs at the Barnum gage over 23 years. Additional details are in the Water Flow chapter.

Mean of daily mean values for each day for 24 years of record in cfs												
Day	Jan	Feb	Mar	Apr	May	Jun	Jul	Aug	Sep	Oct	Nov	Dec
Avg	613	684	1,051	844	603	419	252	224	210	301	413	659

The general conclusion from the 24 year average is that the water is under control between May and November. The rainy months of the spring have the most potential for danger and dictate you check the gage and use caution prior to entering the river. Don't plan your once-in-a-lifetime trip to the North Branch in March!

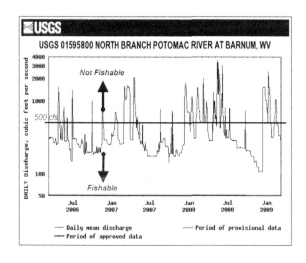

The graph to the left shows the daily flows for the period March 2006 through March 2009 to give you a visual picture of the typical cycle.

Note how quickly the flow can spike from safe to life threatening.

If you are wading, I recommend you not bother when the flow is above 450 cfs. Check with one of the fly shops listed at the back for additional guidance.

Kitzmiller, Lostland and Laurel Run

The Kitzmiller gage is the best downstream from Stony River in the delayed harvest section. I include the historical table that shows the average flow by month and day at the end of the Book.

The good news is you do not have to be sensitive to the releases from the dam in this section or any other section upstream. The water flow through Kitzmiller is a result of natural runoff from the tributaries feeding the river rather than being controlled by human action. But, that's also the bad news since this section does not enjoy the benefits of managed volumes of cold water. If you come here in the summer, you should target smallmouth.

As you can see from the monthly averages, the flow does not get consistently below 400 CFS until the end of May - a date that corresponds with the end of the formal trout stocking program. 400 cfs is my personal preference on the maximum amount of water I want to deal with. While you can fish this area, with caution, at 550 - 600 CFS, *I do not recommend it*. As always, only you can determine the safe level for you since only you know your physical capabilities and limitations. Never enter the water if there is any suspicion that it will be unsafe.

Mean of daily mean values for each day for 41 years of record in cfs												
Day	Jan	Feb	Mar	Apr	May	Jun	Jul	Aug	Sep	Oct	Nov	Dec
Avg	572	672	997	783	529	331	183	180	119	199	306	542

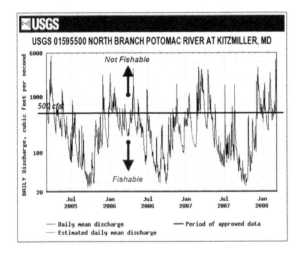

Here is the same three year look as provided for the Barnum gage.

Note how the flow plunges in the middle of summer. At the lower extreme, the river is as unfishable as it is during high flow conditions.

You need at least 50 cfs to visit unless you want to limit your focus to the deeper pools.

Wallman and Gormania

The Steyer Gage is the best to use since both of these areas are upstream of the junction of Stony River with the North Branch. I include the historical table that shows the average flow by month and day at the end of the Book.

As you can review the monthly averages, you might assume this is fishable anytime based on the 550-600 cfs guidance discussed so far. The actual "magic number" is different because the physical characteristics of the river here. As a general rule, 200 cfs is the maximum from the junction of Stony River upstream. Again, you must set your own standards.

Mean of daily mean values for each day for 52 years of record in, cfs												
	Jan	Feb	Mar	Apr	May	Jun	Jul	Aug	Sep	Oct	Nov	Dec
Avg	232	250	342	275	196	121	102	80	63	72	140	214

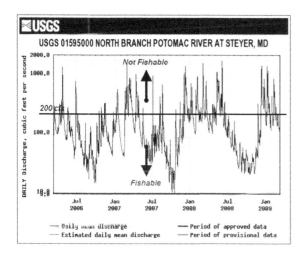

Here is the three year cycle.

As a general statement, Wallman and Gormania are usually fishable.

The huge spike in the spring of 2009 shown on the graph indicates what can happen to the fishing if there is a very wet spring.

Since the dam is not available to ensure consistent flow, you need to be as aware of minimums as you are cautious of maximums. The pictures below were taken when the flow was 28 cfs at Kitzmiller and 14 cfs at the Steyer gage. This shows how bad the upper river can get if there is not enough water. In these conditions, the fish retreat to the deeper pools where they hang on for survival with their fingernails ... if they had some.

Upstream from Lostland Run at 14 cfs (Steyer)

Upstream near Laurel Run at 28 cfs (Kitzmiller)

Wallman

I recommend you not fish here when the flow is over 200 cfs measured at Steyer. The Wallman section is very narrow. This forces the flow into a very tight area that amplifies the significance even when there is limited water elsewhere. You can fish here when flows are as low as 70 cfs and still have a decent day.

Gormania

If you look at the monthly averages, you see the water dries up considerably after May with flows dropping from the May average of 196 cfs to 63 cfs in September. You can fish this section up to 250 cfs, but be very careful above 200 cfs.

Stony River

The Mt Storm gage sits at the upper end of the Stony River near Route 50. The historical table with the average flow by month and day is at the end of the Book.

The Stony River is not part of the North Branch, so it has its own rules. My experience is you can fish this river whenever it is safe to wade across the North Branch. If the North Branch is above the safe level, do not try and fish here. Minimum flow for the Stony is 40 cfs.

Mean of daily mean values for each day for 43 years of record in cfs												
Day	Jan	Feb	Mar	Apr	May	Jun	Jul	Aug	Sep	Oct	Nov	Dec
Avg	114	133	220	160	119	68	48	35	42	45	87	103

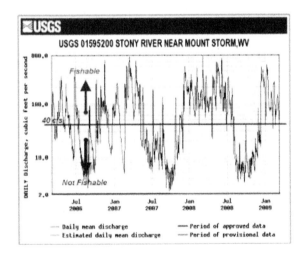

The Stony is a feeder "river" into the North Branch and is fishable above 40 cfs.

Below 40 cfs, your fishing will be confined to widely spread pools.

While the historical temperature record indicates trout may survive up here, it is not stocked and I have not encountered any trout outside of the immediate area of the junction with the North Branch.

Best Time to Fish

It goes without saying that you should check with one of the fly shops if you are going to drive a long distance and are fixated on fishing the North Branch. They will know what the current conditions are beyond what you can divine from one of the gages. If you are not particular, you can head out to Western Maryland and, if it looks bad on the North Branch, flip over to the Savage or hit some wild streams.

Barnum Downstream through Piedmont/Westernport

Since this is a tailwater fishery, it is fishable all year round.

That simple statement is fraught with problems. While it is theoretically fishable year round, the water volume will dictate when it is actually fishable. When you refer to the table above, you see the flow moderates to below 400 cfs in the May/June timeframe and remains good until the winter rains pump the volume up in December. If you fish between December and May, you must check the actual gage reading (Barnum gage) before you drive out. The good news is if the flow is too high here as a result of a human decision to release more water from the dam, you can move upstream above Kitzmiller. However, if you do that, be aware of the water temperature since the water above the dam is hostile to trout holdover in the summer.

Jennings-Randolph Dam

The boat ramp schedules provide the best guidance to the optimum time. While you can fish at the lake all year round, you need a boat to fish it properly. It is the deepest lake in Maryland and reaches an astounding 270 feet in places. The Howell Run Boat Launch in West Virginia opens on April 1 and closes on October 31. On the Maryland side, the Maryland Boat Launch remains open as weather permits. Anglers have caught significant numbers of state record fish in the lake between April and September.

Kitzmiller, Lostland Run, Laurel Run, Wallman, Gormania, Bayard

This is tough as you need to balance three variables:

- Has the river been stocked?
- What is the temperature of the water?
- What is the volume (flow)?

The answer to the stocking question is easy since that occurs in the spring and the fall. Maryland sometimes does a pre-season stocking in February as a lead-in to the normal trout season that runs from March through May. In October and November, the DNR plants additional fish for the late season crowd. The only thing that West Virginia commits to is that their stocking schedule "varies" – they may or may not have added to the fish.

Best Time to Fish
Regulations and property ownership may have changed since publication.
It is your responsibility to know and obey all regulations and not trespass on private property.
11

The temperature is the next variable and is most relevant after May. Unlike the Barnum sections, there is no dam to release chilled water upstream of Bayard to maintain a cold water fishery down through Kitzmiller. Instead, the river water temperature fluctuates based on the amount of rain and sun. In a hot, dry summer, the water ebbs to low levels that allow the sun to heat the water above 80 degrees; killing off the trout. There may be a few survivors huddled around spring seeps, but they will be few and far between.

The good news is that there are smallies here. You can have good days fishing for that tough little species anywhere from the dam upstream. The preferred water temperature for maximum smallmouth activity is between 67 and 71 degrees and they can tolerate warmth that will kill a trout. Interestingly, they are more sensitive to pH (acidity) than trout – so they are the "canaries in the mine" that telegraph water quality trouble. On the other hand, once temperatures plunge below 50 degrees they shut down. Since they need a temperature of at least 60 degrees to spawn, you will not find them in the Barnum tailwater – it stays far too cold.

Sadly, as a result of financial constraints, the USGS stopped showing the temperature on the Kitzmiller gage in 2008 so you need to use the Mount Storm temperature and factor it for the North Branch based on historical averages. The "take away" from these tables are that smallies should be active from March through October. The optimum time for trout is more restricted and does not extend much beyond the spring stocking season. Generally, the North Branch above the dam is fishable for trout from March through July and again as the cool weather sets in late in the year in conjunction with the fall stocking effort.

Official USGS temperature (Kitzmiller - only one year available):

	Jan	Feb	Mar	Apr	May	Jun	Jul	Aug	Sep	Oct	Nov	Dec
Monthly mean in deg C and deg F (Calculation Period: 1993-10-01 -> 1994-09-30)												
C	3.1	2.8	11.1	11.2	13.1	24.7	21.7	20.7	16.9	11.3	5.8	3.6
F	37.6	37.0	52.0	52.2	55.6	76.5	71.1	69.3	62.4	52.3	42.4	38.5

Values I calculated using 5 years of data (Kitzmiller):

Day	Jan	Feb	Mar	Apr	May	Jun	Jul	Aug	Sep	Oct	Nov	Dec
Mean of monthly values for each month for 5 years of record												
Avg F	38.0	35.9	41.9	51.6	58.8	66.7	72.1	72.2	65.6	54.2	45.6	36.7

But, you cannot leap to the conclusion that it is OK to fish here anytime during those months as you must consider the water volume. I will not repeat the extensive discussions from the Water Volume chapter, but you should only fish when the water volume is above the minimum levels and below the danger zone (that will vary based on your personal capabilities – use good judgment). If you have a doubt about the safety of the water, then there is no doubt…. don't fish.

Stony River

The Stony is a marginal fishery as a result of acid runoff. It's worth fishing the Stony if you are in the Wallman area, have some extra time, are curious to see some new water and want to catch a smallmouth near the junction. Therefore, it's a target between March and October. You should regard catching trout in this stream a bonus.

The Mt Storm gage shows temperature as well as gage height and flow and offers the promise of optimum temperature ranges for trout. Unfortunately, the only trout you can expect to find in this stretch are holdovers that migrate up from the North Branch.

Monthly mean in deg C (Calculation Period: 2001-10-01 -> 2007-09-30)												
Year	Jan	Feb	Mar	Apr	May	Jun	Jul	Aug	Sep	Oct	Nov	Dec
Avg C	4.7	4.1	8.0	12.2	16.5	19.2	21.3	21.4	18.6	12.3	9.6	4.8
Avg F	40.5	39.4	46.4	54.0	61.7	66.6	70.3	70.5	65.5	54.1	49.3	40.6

Understanding the Rating System

Every fisherman looks at a body of water in a way that matches their background and personal ideal for what constitutes the perfect fishing experience. I am no different. To fully understand the comments I make in this guide, you need to understand how I evaluate water. The rating tables below provide the criteria I use in deciding whether a particular stretch was worth the effort to get there.

I provide ratings for both a "normal perspective" and an "aggressive perspective". The difference between the two is the amount of adversity you are willing to tolerate to get to a spot.

An aggressive fisherman welcomes a challenging hike, bushwhacking through nasty terrain and having to use a topo map (that is why I include USGS topo map extracts) to find their way to water.

The normal person is probably the opposite of this. Therefore, I provide standard ratings on things that are common – like fish size, pressure, and other typical factors. For access, hard to find and physical fitness, I provide different criteria as described below.

I rate each location against both sets so you can pick the one that matches your preferences.

I need to put a strong disclaimer in at this point.

Physical fitness ratings are based on my impression of what it takes to get to the fishing area and enjoy it. Something I consider challenging may be easy for you or, on the other end of the scale, impossible based on your personal physical situation. *You should never attempt to fish in any spot where taking that step off the bank would put you at risk.* Just because I did not think a particular place was overly taxing physically may not mean much until you match your abilities with mine.

Please re-read and agree to the liability disclaimer on page 2 of the book before you read further.

The table below lays out the standard criteria:

Standard Ratings		
Pressure	**Green**	Saw a few other people
	Yellow	Saw other people, but never felt pressured
	Red	Felt crowded
Scenery	**Green**	Classic trout water of rushing stream with rocks, no houses; for bass, nice wooded lake
	Yellow	Trout - Flatter water, but still remote; bass water has houses overlooking the lake or river
	Red	Boring, populated
Trout Size	**Green**	Trout - 14" or larger
	Yellow	Trout - 10" or larger
	Red	Trout - smaller than 10" or not present
Bass Size	**Green**	Bass - 14"
	Yellow	Bass - 10"
	Red	Bass - smaller than 10" or not present
Regulations	**Green**	Catch and Release or a slot for bass
	Yellow	Delayed Harvest
	Red	Put and Take
Stocking	**Green**	Stocked
	Yellow	N/A - not used
	Red	Not Stocked
Overall	**Green**	I would come back anytime
	Yellow	Would go if I don't have anywhere better to go
	Red	Will not come back

Normal Perspective Criteria:

Normal Perspective		
Physical Fitness	**Green**	Normal level of fitness required
	Yellow	Suitable for somebody who exercises often and is in reasonable shape
	Red	Suitable for somebody who is in good shape
Access	**Green**	Easy access. Well-marked trail follows the stream. If this is a lake, the boat ramp can take a normal sized bass boat
	Yellow	Some trail, but not consistent - comes and goes. Boat ramp suitable for light boats only
	Red	No trail, you are in the river wading; no boat ramp - you have to drag your boat to the water.
Hard to find	**Green**	Easy to get there. Google Maps will get you to the right spot; hardball road all the way
	Yellow	Involves traveling on a dirt road for a portion; you need to pay attention or you may take the wrong turn
	Red	Requires that you read a topo map

Aggressive Perspective Criteria:

Aggressive Perspective		
Physical Fitness	**Green**	Suitable for somebody who is in good shape
	Yellow	Suitable for somebody who exercises often and is in reasonable shape
	Red	Normal level of fitness required
Access	**Green**	No trail, you are in the river wading; no boat ramp - you have to drag your boat to the water.
	Yellow	Some trail, but not consistent - comes and goes. Boat ramp suitable for light boats only
	Red	Easy access. Well-marked trail follows the stream. If this is a lake, the boat ramps can take a normal sized bass boat
Hard to find	**Green**	Requires that you read a topo map
	Yellow	Involves traveling on a dirt road for a portion; you need to pay attention or you may take the wrong turn
	Red	Easy to get there. Google Maps will get you to the right spot; hardball road all the way

Overall Rating Summary

The specifics behind these ratings are in the individual sections. Here are my conclusions "up front" as a consolidated reference.

Normal Perspective

	Low Pressure	Easy Physical Fitness	Easy Access	Easy to Find	Scenery	Trout Size	Bass Size	Regs	Stocking	Overall
Piedmont	Red	Green	Green	Green	Red	Green	Red	Red	Green	Yellow
Bloomington	Green	Red	Red	Green	Yellow	Green	Red	Green	Green	Red
Barnum Upper (North)	Red	Yellow	Green	Yellow	Green	Green	Red	Green	Green	Green
Barnum Put and Take	Red	Green	Green	Yellow	Green	Green	Red	Red	Green	Yellow
Barnum Lower (South)	Red	Yellow	Green	Green	Green	Green	Red	Green	Green	Green
Paul Sarbanes Trail	Green	Red	Green	Yellow	Green	Green	Red	Green	Green	Green
Jennings Randolph	Red	Green	Green	Green	Green	Green	Green	Red	Green	Green
Kitzmiller	Green	Red	Red	Green	Green	Yellow	Yellow	Red	Green	Yellow
Lostland Run	Green	Red	Yellow	Yellow	Green	Green	Yellow	Yellow	Green	Green
Laurel Run	Red	Yellow	Red	Red	Green	Green	Yellow	Yellow	Green	Yellow
Wallman	Green	Green	Yellow	Red	Green	Green	Yellow	Yellow	Green	Green
Stony River	Green	Red	Yellow	Red	Green	Red	Yellow	Red	Red	Red
Gormania	Red	Green	Yellow	Green	Yellow	Green	Yellow	Red	Green	Yellow
Bayard	Red	Green	Green	Green	Red	Green	Red	Red	Green	Red

Aggressive Perspective

Location	Low Pressure	Tough Physical Fitness	Hard Access	Hard to Find	Scenery	Trout Size	Bass Size	Regs	Stocking	Overall
Piedmont	Red	Red	Red	Red	Red	Green	Red	Red	Green	Red
Bloomington	Green	Green	Green	Red	Yellow	Green	Red	Green	Green	Green
Barnum Upper (North)	Red	Yellow	Red	Yellow	Green	Green	Red	Green	Green	Yellow
Barnum Put and Take	Red	Red	Red	Yellow	Green	Green	Red	Red	Green	Red
Barnum Lower (South)	Red	Yellow	Red	Red	Green	Green	Red	Green	Green	Yellow
Paul Sarbanes Trail	Green	Green	Green	Yellow	Green	Green	Red	Green	Green	Green
Jennings Randolph	Red	Red	Red	Red	Green	Green	Green	Red	Green	Yellow
Kitzmiller	Green	Green	Green	Red	Green	Yellow	Yellow	Red	Green	Yellow
Lostland Run	Green	Green	Yellow	Yellow	Green	Green	Yellow	Yellow	Green	Green
Laurel Run	Red	Yellow	Green	Green	Green	Green	Yellow	Yellow	Green	Yellow
Wallman	Green	Red	Yellow	Green	Green	Green	Yellow	Yellow	Green	Green
Stony River	Green	Green	Yellow	Green	Green	Red	Yellow	Red	Red	Yellow
Gormania	Red	Red	Yellow	Red	Yellow	Green	Yellow	Red	Green	Red
Bayard	Red	Red	Red	Red	Red	Green	Red	Red	Green	Red

Piedmont/Westernport

Summary Rating

Normal Perspective

Pressure	**Red**	Trout Size	**Green**
Physical Fitness	**Green**	Bass Size	**Red**
Access	**Green**	Regulations	**Red**
Hard to Find	**Green**	Stocking	**Green**
Scenery	**Red**	**Overall**	**Yellow**

Aggressive Perspective

Pressure	**Red**	Trout Size	**Green**
Physical Fitness	**Red**	Bass Size	**Red**
Access	**Red**	Regulations	**Red**
Hard to Find	**Red**	Stocking	**Green**
Scenery	**Red**	**Overall**	**Red**

Special Regulations

None. This is a "Put and Take" section running from Piney Swamp Run to the west of Bloomington downstream (the river runs north) to the Upper Potomac River Commission Wastewater Treatment Plant discharge in Westernport.

Below (downstream) of that point, the North Branch is a zero creel limit (you cannot keep anything), catch and release only body of water to the Route 956 bridge at Pinto for trout. For bass, the zero creel limit, catch and return regulation applies from the Route 220 bridge at Keyser downstream approximately 25 miles to the spillway in Cumberland.

I'll be upfront. The Piedmont and Bayard sections form the horrible bookends to a great, scenic river. I include a discussion of both of these areas for completeness, but they both lack any redeeming characteristics other than being stocked.

Getting to the Stream

Navigate to Westernport, MD.

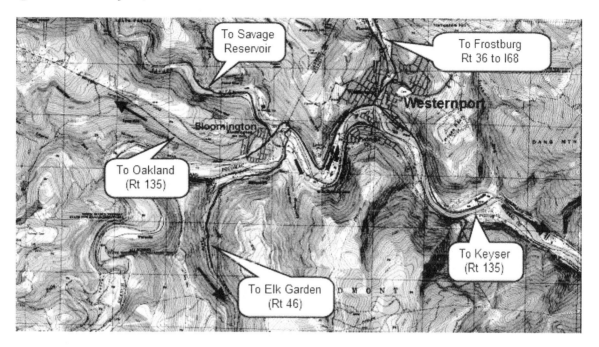

Access Points:
- Westernport:
  - Parking lot near the ball field on 1st Street (39.481135,-79.04396)
  - Dirt parking lot behind the sign for the Westernport Railroad Park on Front Street (39.48364,-79.04602)
- Piedmont: Parking lot on River Lane (39.483268,-79.048761)
- Luke: Side of the road on MD 135 (39.474921,-79.061316, 39.480065,-79.065549)

This is a pretty nasty looking spot. You get to "enjoy" the sights and smell associated with the Westvaco Paper plant that is the big black blob in the center of the map.

In fact, I do not recommend fishing in this section as there are better places both up and downstream. Piedmont offers true urban fishing where you can park, fish, move your car, fish, and move again. You always have a landmark to use as reference with the dense white smoke billowing out of the paper plant. The water is not clear until you get above the junction of the Savage River with the North Branch.

Downstream, the Zero Creel area offers more interesting fishing. It is not stocked, but the cold water out of the Jennings-Randolph and Savage River dams create good habitat for wild trout and the stocked fish that migrate downstream. The farther downstream you go, the deeper it gets, so be careful if you decide to wade and pay attention to private property – access the river only at the boat launch.

Environment and Fish

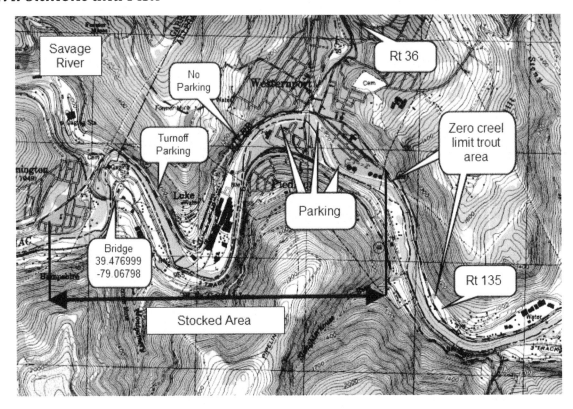

Westernport and Piedmont would actually be pretty little towns if it were not for the Westvaco paper mill belching huge quantities of white, thick smoke into the air just upstream in Luke. That said, this is stocked trout water and you can fish here. The stocked area begins at the wastewater treatment plant at the east end of Westernport and extends upstream to the start of the Barnum catch and release area south of Bloomington.

The first place to fish is to turn south onto Maryland Avenue from Route 135 and follow it to 1st Street. Turn right on 1st Street. As you drive by the baseball field on the left, the road goes on top of a high berm allowing you to see the river to the right. The big tanks of the wastewater treatment plant loom to your front hidden behind a small stand of trees. Follow the road and pull off just before the gate at the entrance of the plant. There's a well-defined path to take you to the river. As you look at the river from the road, you discover you are at the junction of two forks. The large body of land in front of you is actually a long skinny island separating the main stem of the river from a sidebar. You can fish up either and pursue the stocked fish.

Farther upstream, you encounter your next access point - the unimproved boat launch at the intersection of Route 135 and Maryland Avenue. You have to look hard to find the launch as there are no signs pointing you to it from the road. At the junction, look for a small granite sign for the Westernport Railroad Park on the other side of the railroad tracks and locate the dirt road on the right. The road immediately bumps down a steep hill into an extended parking area at 39.483694,-79.045987. This is the junction of Georges Creek with the North Branch.

You can walk down Georges Creek to the river or cut west overland to access the North Branch. From here, you can fish upstream underneath the bridge with the town of Piedmont on your left. The river is wide and shallow in this area at normal flows from both the Savage and Jennings Randolph Dams. If you really want to fish here, a better option is to go across the river on Route 46, turn right on 3rd Street and follow it to its dead-end on Orchard Street.

Turn right on Orchard and park at the junction of Orchard and Riverside Lane. Here, it's an easy, quick walk down a short, steep hill to the river. Assuming no "no parking" signs have sprouted since publication, this is the last place you'll be to obtain access until you move upstream of the paper mill. Between Piedmont and Luke on Route 135 there are no safe turnoffs and no easy access to the river. As you fish upstream from Riverside Lane, the river remains wide and shallow until it narrows closer to the plant. I do not recommend spending much time here because of the less than attractive environment and the pervasive smell of the paper plant.

A better option is to continue on Route 135 until it begins to parallel the river on the east side of Luke. The river forms a deep, long lake that is stocked and holds fish. Granted, you have a close view of the paper plant to your left but it is worth fishing if you can use spin gear. Your access to the river is facilitated by a large number of turnouts along Route 135 where you can push your way through some scraggly bushes down the short bank to the water. There is no room for a backcast, making it rough for fly fishing. As you look out into the river, there are large numbers of submerged boulders and other structure supplying good holding areas for fish. When you leave the lake heading upstream, you begin to see more riffled areas interspersed with boulders and whitewater. This is the start of the hard wading the North Branch is famous for; a unique coating of slime coats every rock in sight. Armed with your wading staff, you can fish upstream and, as long as you do not look back towards Luke, it starts to become scenic.

Most people park at the intersection of Route 46 and Route 135 or upstream a bit where Route 135 crosses the Savage River. If you go to Google™ Maps and turn on the satellite view at 39.479823,-79.066865, you can see the complex jumble of cuts and jogs in the combined course of the two rivers that make for interesting fishing.

The other access point is from Bloomington. Once on Route 135 heading towards Oakland, make your first left turn on Hamill Ave. Take an immediate left onto Owens Ave and follow it through the stop sign down a steep hill. There's a broad turnaround at the bottom of the hill where you can park. Walk around the stand of trees on the left to the bridge. This is a popular takeout spot for kayakers who come down the North Branch from the Barnum area. There are usually portable toilets here if you need to use them.

Piedmont/Westernport

Regulations and property ownership may have changed since publication.
It is your responsibility to know and obey all regulations and not trespass on private property.

21

View from the Water Treatment plant looking upstream from 39.479632,-79.042983

The land on the left is an island. You can fish up either side.

The greater flow is on the west side of the island.

View upstream from the parking area off Riverside Lane at 39.483011,-79.049399 (look for any no parking signs in case they have sprouted since publication).

The river is shallow. This is where you need to park if you want to fish upstream to the paper plant.

Flow was 241 cfs at Barnum when I took this picture.

The paper plant throws plenty of smoke and odor into the air. This is not a nice section to fish.

This picture looks downstream from one of the many parking spots off of Route 135 upstream of Luke (39.475608,-79.061866)

The river is very deep – you will not be able to wade and the dense trees on the bank dictate you use spin gear.

The farther upstream you move from the paper plant, the more normal the river becomes.

This is the junction of the Savage River with the North Branch looking upstream on the North Branch from 39.480875,-79.067402. You can begin to wade here.

If you fish the Savage River, be aware of the special regulations in effect.

The railroad bridge at 39.476949,-79.068003 is a popular spot.

The bridge offers a set of very deep holes and is the last easy place for the stocking truck to plant fish in the river.

You can wade upstream from here into the catch and release area discussed in the next section. This is also the take-out for kayakers.

Bottom line

This is not a scenic spot. If you just want to get a quick "road fishing" fix as you drive by, it's fine for that. Head over to the spot upstream from Luke and throw some spinners, small crankbaits or even some worms on a slip bobber and have some fun. But, don't plan a family picnic there!

A better spot for "Put and Take" is in Barnum itself. It's only a 20 minute drive south and you get good fish action in a scenic setting.

Bloomington

Summary Rating

Normal Perspective

Pressure	**Green**	Trout Size	**Green**
Physical Fitness	**Red**	Bass Size	**Red**
Access	**Red**	Regulations	**Green**
Hard to Find	**Green**	Stocking	**Green**
Scenery	**Yellow**	Overall	**Red**

Aggressive Perspective

Pressure	**Green**	Trout Size	**Green**
Physical Fitness	**Green**	Bass Size	**Red**
Access	**Green**	Regulations	**Green**
Hard to Find	**Red**	Stocking	**Green**
Scenery	**Yellow**	Overall	**Green**

Special Regulations

Be careful here. The "Put and Take" section begins at the entrance of Piney Swamp Run and extends down to Westernport. That section allows a daily / possession creel limit of 5 trout. The section covered in this discussion is UPSTREAM from Piney Swamp Run and *falls into the Catch and Return portion* of the river that begins 4 miles farther south just below the spot known as the "Blue Hole".

The regulations restrict you to artificial lures and flies. Those artificial lures must be unscented and you cannot apply scent to unscented lures. Bait is expressly prohibited in this area.

Getting to the Stream

Navigate to Bloomington, MD.

Access Points:
- Kayak takeout at the end of Owens Avenue (39.476311,-79.06942)
- Small lot on Seldom Seen Road off MD 135 (39.474415,-79.076694)

As you drive south on MD 135 from the bridge, turn left onto Seldom Seen Road and park at the iron bar gate in the wide spot to the left of the gate. There is only room for one or two trucks here. The "parking area" is directly behind an apartment building and only a short distance from the turn off of MD 135. At some point, this access my be restricted, so look for any "no parking" signs before you leave your vehicle.

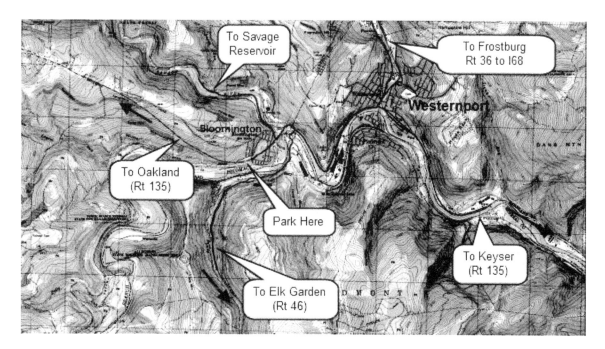

Walk on the road until you decide to cut over to the stream. The road moves away from the river, so make your move before it starts to follow the hill that looms high above the river unless you want to walk to the bend and begin fishing there.

The first time I came here, I was optimistic that Seldom Seen Road would allow vehicle access all the way into the heart of the catch and release area. If you look at the map, you can see it extends deep into the back section. With the gate firmly locked, that hope was destroyed.

If you want to fish the "Put and Take" area below Piney Swamp Run, you should go to the kayak takeout just upstream of the bridge (39.476949,-79.068003) and start fishing there. It's about a mile from that point to Piney Swamp Run. Another alternative is that you can walk to the intersection of Seldom Seen Road and the railroad. Turn left and follow the tracks (do not walk on the tracks) back down to the river. That will be a ½ mile walk, but you will move faster than wading up the river.

But the real reason to come to this spot is to fish the catch and release section. You have two options.

Option 1: Be prepared to deal with the underbrush. As you walk past the intersection of Seldom Seen Road with the rail bed, start looking for a good place to cut to the river – there is no beaten trail. The easiest place is after passing a fenced area (39.473546,-79.08652) you can see in this picture.

Follow the ravine on the west side of the fence through some heavy undergrowth to emerge at the river bank opposite of Piney Swamp Run.

Option 2: Follow the road and stay off the railroad. The road dips down in the valley and eventually climbs back up the hill to parallel the railroad track. Follow it down the long steep hill. After a 0.4 mile, it bottoms out in the valley near a sharp bend in the river. From this point (39.477239,-79.101895), it's an easy walk through the underbrush to the water.

Environment and Fish

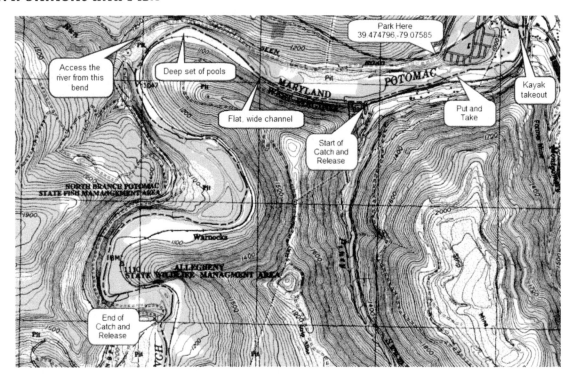

The primary species of fish here is trout – brook, brown, cutthroat and rainbow thrive in the cold water discharge from the Jennings-Randolph Dam. In fact, trout can be found many miles below Westernport because of the reinforcing effect of equally cold water from the Savage River joining the North Branch at Bloomington. There are no smallmouth bass between Piedmont and the Jennings-Randolph Dam because of the cool water stays below the 60 degree temperature for required for spawning.

The river starts out flat and wide at the beginning of the catch and release area. During high water in the spring, it will flow fast and deep; something confirmed by the water marks carved onto the high southern bank. There are plenty of rocks and boulders breaking up the water and providing good holding cover for trout. A heavy coat of North Branch slime coats all the rocks and demands cautious wading. The scenery is typical North Branch except for the early portion where you can still see and smell the activity down in Luke and Bloomington, which is why this earns a "Yellow" for the scenery category.

The high, steep hill on the southern bank tucks the old (inactive) rail bed tight into its lower slope and offers a high speed, fast track if you want to use it to get upstream. On the northern side, the terrain is equally as steep after you pass the fenced area. Once you get into the water and start fishing upstream, you will move away from any easy escape route. Be prepared to hump up a very steep hill or move all the way to the bend for a gentler exit. It's a 1.5 mile walk back out from the bend.

The southern bank shelters a series of good spots that have the most depth. The gradient of the river moves quickly from deep to shallow as you traverse from south to north. The southern bank is abrupt and tight against the steep hill while the northern bank features the broad rock farms associated with a shallow bank that quickly transition into a steep hill mirroring the one on the other side. This continues as you move west.

The river narrows as it comes out of the upstream bend and the steep cliff face closes out access from the northern bank. This same structure creates a beautiful ¼ mile narrow, deep channel to easily absorb your total attention for more than an hour. The best structure in the channel is next to the northern bank and there are also large boulders scattered throughout the stretch that provide targets for your efforts. To fish this effectively, you need to go deep. A sink tip or full sinking line is an advantage here. If you use spin gear, you should weight your spinners with split shot to get them deep quickly. Otherwise, the fast current will whip them downstream over the top of the fish.

As you round the corner, the river returns to a flat, open character. It is not shallow, but is wadeable. The next ¼ mile upstream is fast, rushing water pressing through deep cuts. You must pick your course carefully as the water compresses and increases velocity down the moderate gradient. The boulder strewn bottom is perfect habitat for the wild trout.

If you want to move quickly upstream, you can do it here by crossing and hopping on the wide path that used to be the railroad track leading to the mining town of Warnocks.

On the northern bank, if you do not want to fish the pools at the bend, continue on Seldom Seen Road. It breaks into a small open field that is your last easy opportunity to access the river. Cut across the field and move through any of the openings to walk to the river. The river tightens up at this end of the bend before it turns south into the long flat section leading to the area discussed in the next chapter. As a general rule, I recommend you abandon Seldom Seen Road at the pools near the bend, cross the river and use the old railroad track leading to Warnock as your primary trail.

Since this area is at the extreme northern end of the northern Barnum catch and release area, it is unlikely that you will see anyone else here. The 1.5 mile walk in from Bloomington is easier than the 2.5 mile walk from the south.

This is the view upstream from the option 1 entry point at the bottom of the ravine just past the fenced area.

The river is broad and flat with a few boulders poking up here and there.

The deeper section is on the southern shore. You can see from the boulder field at the right of the picture that the gradient slopes to the left (south towards West Virginia).

Looking downstream from the option 1 entry point.

Mud and muck protect much of the northern bank in this area.

Be careful when you enter the stream. You can sink up to your knees if you are not careful when you step off the bank.

This is the road that leads to the option 2 entry point. It takes a long, gentle angle down the steep slope to the river

With the leaves off the trees, you can see the broad sweep of the river upstream.

This is far enough from the normal Barnum southern access point that this section does not get much pressure.

This picture shows the rock structure at the upstream start of the long, deep pool section at the bend in the river.

The only way to fish this is to go to the bottom and cross the river.

The view upstream from the option 2 entry point at 39.476949,-79.101541.

There are numerous deep channels spread across this section. You may have to move up or downstream to find a spot to cross. Be very, very careful if you wade across the river. It is VERY fast here.

The Barnum gage was running at 241 cfs when I took this picture and wading was tough.

The level spot on the left is the old rail to Warnocks.

The view downstream from the option 2 entry point.

Cross (if it is safe) and move down the right hand bank to get to the cliff area at the top center of the picture.

Fish your way downstream – there are plenty of good spots.

This picture looks upstream into the pool area.

Note the steep bank on the right (north) side. The water runs shallow to deep from left to right. The deepest spots are next to the cliff face.

The velocity of the current is quick here.

Once you fish the broad, flat area upstream of the option 2 entry point, the river completes its turn around the bend.

Picture taken looking downstream from 39.47504,-79.10506

The vegetation is dense on the north bank. Fish from the south bank.

View into the start of the bend leading to the northern Barnum catch and release area.

The river is very tight here as you can see from the whitewater. Be careful.

The smooth, flat rail bed leading south is at the upper left in this picture.

Bottom Line

The character of this water is good and "trouty". However, the scenery is bland in the lower portion when compared to what you will encounter farther upstream. Given the demanding walk to get into and the climb out of this section, it is not heavily pressured. Do not walk on the active railbed on the north bank.

Barnum North C&R

Summary Rating

Normal Perspective

Pressure	**Red**	Trout Size	**Green**
Physical Fitness	**Yellow**	Bass Size	**Red**
Access	**Green**	Regulations	**Green**
Hard to Find	**Yellow**	Stocking	**Green**
Scenery	**Green**	**Overall**	**Green**

Aggressive Perspective

Pressure	**Red**	Trout Size	**Green**
Physical Fitness	**Yellow**	Bass Size	**Red**
Access	**Red**	Regulations	**Green**
Hard to Find	**Yellow**	Stocking	**Green**
Scenery	**Green**	**Overall**	**Yellow**

Special Regulations

Only use artificial lures and flies. Those artificial lures must be unscented and you cannot apply scent to unscented lures. Bait is expressly prohibited in this area.

Getting to the Stream

From the South: Navigate to Elk Garden, WV. At Elk Garden, turn north on Route 46. That road will take you past the lake, the dam and eventually intersects with Barnum Road. Turn left on Barnum Road (Co Hwy 46/2).

From the North: Navigate to Westernport, MD. Follow Route 135 west out of Westernport towards Luke. On the other side of Luke, you must turn left (south) on Route 46. Route 46 will eventually intersect with Barnum Road (Co Hwy 46/2). Turn right on Barnum Road.

There is a church at the intersection of Route 46 and Barnum Road.

Barnum Road will take you right to the river. When you hit the river, you will be in the south parking area. Visit the nice public toilets here if you have to and then continue up the dirt road (heading north). Follow the road until it dead-ends in a large parking lot.

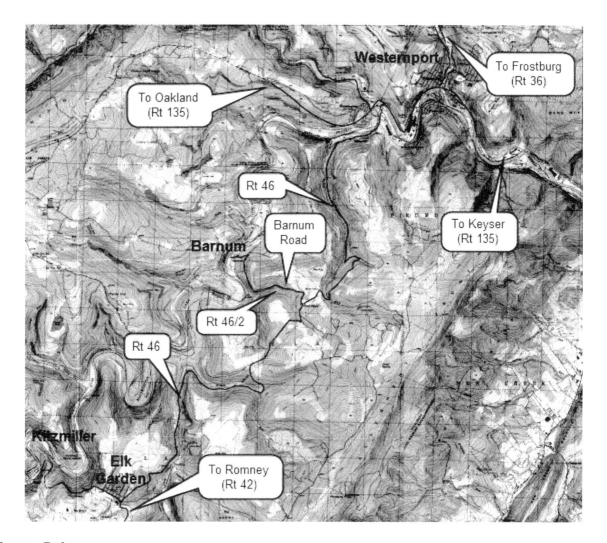

Access Point:
- Parking lot at the Blue Hole (39.455182,-79.101866)

Before you walk over to the trail, go to the west end of the parking lot where there is a gap in the trees and look downstream. This is the famous "Blue Hole"- a spot that gets hammered by folks who sometimes stand shoulder to shoulder; all fishing hard.

There is a red post and a cable across the river downstream marking the start of the special regulation area.

Once you check this out, the trail to the catch and release area is at the northern end of the parking lot. It is a wide path that used to be the railroad into the mining town of Warnock.

Barnum North C&R

Regulations and property ownership may have changed since publication.
It is your responsibility to know and obey all regulations and not trespass on private property.

33

Environment and Fish

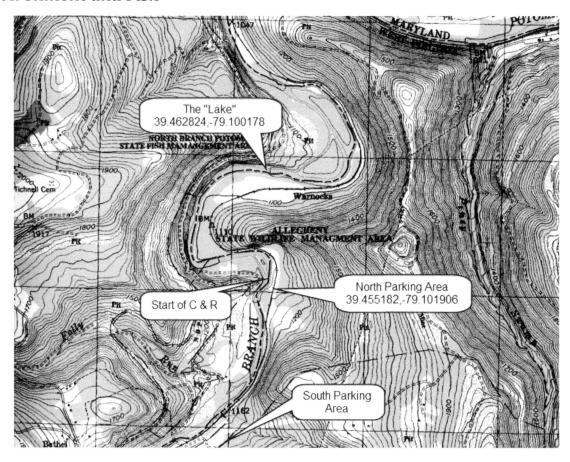

This section of the North Branch offers a scenery trifecta. It's wide, deep and tight; sometimes all of the above in the same section. There are plenty of runs and pools that are too deep to wade and force you to the side of the river. You have to pick your crossings carefully as a result of the strong surge of water and scarcity of shallow areas during times of normal flow.

Working downstream from south to north, you encounter a medium wide section downstream of the Blue Hole with a deep cut on the eastern bank near a large concrete wall (you can see it on the satellite view) followed by a quick transition around the corner into a narrow stretch. While narrow, it remains deep enough to require careful wading.

On the other side of the small cemetery tucked in the bend, the river widens out. Adjacent to the cemetery, there is a cliff face with a deep pool that spins downstream into a fast, wide section that runs about 2 – 3 feet deep terminating in a boulder field and a moderate gradient change adding velocity to the water. The fast section feeds into what I call the "lake" in the vicinity of 39.46325, -79.10443. After the lake, stay to the east and follow the main channel downstream. There are fish all over the place - if you can figure out how to catch them. The Maryland DNR only stocks fingerlings in this section, so all these guys are wild and wary.

Once you are in the parking lot, walk to the gate at the northeast corner and proceed down this well-defined trail.

This is the old rail bed into the town of Warnock.

As you follow the trail, this will be the first place where you break back out into the sun (39.457775,-79.104255). The parking lot is upstream about 50 yards from where I took this picture.

This is a good spot to fish. At the base of the concrete wall, there is a very deep, fast run. You can stand on the top and watch the trout down below. I've seen a lot of guys fishing here, but never seen anyone catch one of those smart fish.

On all my visits except for one, there has always been somebody sitting in this spot, clinging precariously to the concrete as they try and cast. They uniformly attack the deep cut from the concrete side; having slid down where the trail breaks out of the trees. I believe you will have better luck if you fish this from the far bank as you will be less visible to the monsters hovering here. To get to the far bank, you can either bushwhack through the brush and cross at the upstream corner or go downstream to where the river cuts around the bend and look for a spot to wade.

Upstream from the lake, cut around the curve and the river will look like this.

It's narrower, faster and has plenty of rocks to create transition areas holding fish.

Upstream, this leads into the section near the cemetery.

The lake section (39.46325, -79.10443). It is shallow enough to wade on the right (east) side. It's DEEP here. You can't get out that far.

This is where you need to use a sink tip to dredge the bottom. You can attach one to your floating line, but it would be a better strategy to bring a real sinking line.

The big browns huddle on the bottom.

Looking upstream (south) from 39.468469,-79.099288 around the bend from the lake.

The river is fast and medium width at this point.

You cannot see it in the picture, but there are two three foot deep channels where the trout hang out.

Float a nymph or twitch a streamer down those channels to pick up some good fish.

Looking downstream (north) from 39.468469,-79.099288.

The river broadens and gains some speed. The bank is steep and you need to be careful as you select your entry point.

On the other (west) side of the river, the bank has a gentle gradient where it joins the river. Use it to move upstream to get around the deep spots that close you out on the eastern side.

Bottom line

Considering the number of fishermen I encountered, it is pressured. Walking away from the road does not ensure a solitary experience. There are plenty of hardy fishermen who welcome the opportunity to take a good walk into the woods and jump in a cold river on a hot summer day. The interest is heightened by the opportunity to catch wild, trophy size brown or rainbow trout. Add to that the catch and release ethic coupled with spectacular scenery and you have a combination that is hard to beat. The best way to avoid the crowd is to fish during the week. Get here early and take the long walk down the path until your fishing addiction forces you to the river.

Barnum Put and Take

Summary Rating

Normal Perspective

Pressure	Red	Trout Size	Green
Physical Fitness	Green	Bass Size	Red
Access	Green	Regulations	Red
Hard to Find	Yellow	Stocking	Green
Scenery	Green	**Overall**	Yellow

Aggressive Perspective

Pressure	Red	Trout Size	Green
Physical Fitness	Red	Bass Size	Red
Access	Red	Regulations	Red
Hard to Find	Yellow	Stocking	Green
Scenery	Green	**Overall**	Red

Special Regulations

This section is subject to "Put and Take" regulations that apply from the concrete abutments upstream of the south parking lot downstream to just past the Blue Hole – about 1.25 miles.

You can use any type of gear, including bait, in this section

Getting to the Stream

From the South: Navigate to Elk Garden, WV. At Elk Garden, turn north on Route 46. That road will take you past the lake, the dam and eventually intersects with Barnum Road. Turn left on Barnum Road (Co Hwy 46/2).

From the North: Navigate to Westernport, MD. Follow Route 135 west out of Westernport towards Luke. On the other side of Luke, you must turn left (south) on Route 46. Route 46 eventually intersects with Barnum Road (Co Hwy 46/2). Turn right on Barnum Road.

There is a church at the intersection of Route 46 and Barnum Road.

Barnum Road will take you right to the river. When you hit the river, you will be in the south parking area. Visit the nice public toilets here if you have to and then continue up the dirt road (heading north).

The "Put and Take" area is perfect for those who cannot walk any distance to get to the river since the road parallels the river for the majority of this section. However, the eastern bank supporting the road is very steep at the northern end and you have to be nimble and cautious to get down to the water. Be careful and choose your spot well. Once you are next to the stream, you should find a place to cross so you can move up and down the river. There is no room to walk on the eastern bank in the middle/northern section as a result of the sharp drop from the road.

You can obtain easier access to the river in the southern portion near the parking lot or upstream from the Blue Hole. See the large, detailed map in the previous section for additional directions.

Access Points:
- Parking lot near the river (39.442503,-79.114427)
- Various narrow turnouts along the road
- Parking lot at the Blue Hole (39.455182,-79.101866)

Environment and Fish

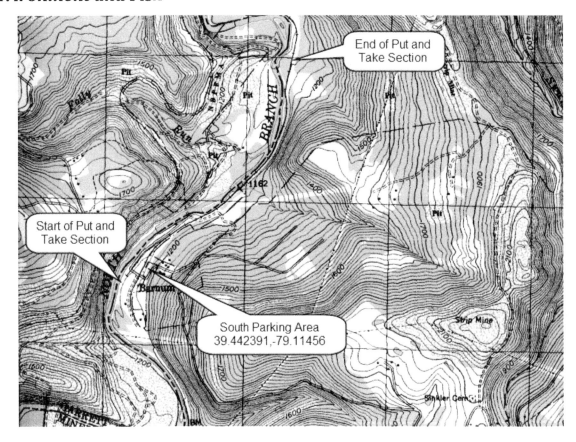

The "Put and Take" area is one of the more scenic sections on an exceptionally scenic river. The river narrows here; piling huge amounts of water into a very small space. This makes wading, particularity crossing the river, a sporty undertaking requiring the careful exercise of good judgment.

Working upstream from the Blue Hole, the river alternates between wide and narrow but remains uniformly deep. After tumbling down a slight slope into the Blue Hole, the river spreads into a broad lake with the deep channel on the east (road) side. After this calm area, it takes an expansive sweep to the east with an extended rough section of scattered boulders and fast current.

Midway through, there is a brief respite where the river becomes more accessible thanks to a rocky bank stretching out from the road; providing a brief opportunity to get to the water without climbing down a steep bank.

Farther upstream and until the road veers away from the river to make space for a series of campsites, the bank is steep; demanding caution as well as restricting your ability to fly fish from the east bank. Once into the camping area, the bank widens; extending smoothly up from the water's edge to the road.

Throughout this section, you will find a natural segregation occurring based on the type of fishing you are interested in. The spin and bait fishermen huddle around the deep runs and lakes; generally fishing right from the roadside. There is no room for a fly fisherman's backcast here and even less room for safe movement – once you are down from the road, you have to sit and fish right there.

The fly fishermen move away from the road and concentrate on the parts of the river featuring more rapid water where it flows down small gradient breaks; creating small sprays of whitewater bordering cuts running three or more feet deep. There is no opportunity for a spinner to work effectively in this water; the velocity pushes these lures quickly downstream denying them the opportunity to start their action.

The "Put and Take" section is generally narrower than what you encounter farther downstream. Particularly, as the river enters the northern end, the high mountain on the east bank creates a narrow passage compressing the water and forcing an increase in velocity. If you are looking for a gentler experience, focus on the southern area where the gradient is more moderate.

West Virginia has a number of campsites you can rent right along the river. Each features a picnic table and fire ring.

This is the famous Blue Hole.

It is absolutely hammered, but also gets more than its fair share of stocked fish.

If you look closely, you can see a number of folks perched on the bank working this area hard.

The catch and release area is downstream of this spot.

Upstream of the Blue Hole looking north at 39.45289,-79.10247

The river is flat, wide and deep in this section. It is tough to fish from the bank next to the road. You have to climb down and find a place to perch on the rocks.

There is no room for a backcast; bring spin gear unless you fish from the west bank.

The "Put and Take" section is moderate width; running 40 – 50 feet in most places.

It is tight and fast with the water pushing strongly downstream over well-spaced rapids.

This picture looks upstream in the northern portion of the "Put and Take" section at approximately 39.44918, 79.10348

Just upstream, you see the typical pattern of gradient breaks with small amounts of whitewater.

Note the deeply submerged rocks in the center. Fish the channels on either side of these and you will catch fish.

You will not be able to wade across the river here – you need to go up to the riffles and it will be tough there as well because of the compression of the water into a tight space.

Looking downstream from that same spot.

The river broadens a bit and transitions to a smooth, fast flow.

Picture taken from the road looking downstream near 39.45055, 79.10279

The key points are the elevation of the road above the river and the nice rock structure that repeats as the river breaks out into the wide area above the Blue Hole.

The river narrows farther downstream as it enters the Blue Hole

Typical rock island.

Here, these provide a welcome spot to get out of the cold water yet still provide a place where you can work some good runs.

When the river breaks out of the southern, flat area, it parallels the road (road is on the right). Upstream from here, you can work the east bank easily; downstream, it is steep and restrictive.

From here north, the deep section is typically on the eastern bank.

Picture looking north from 39.44654,-79.10707

Picture looking south from 39.44654,-79.10707 as it enters the flatter southern area of the "Put and Take" section.

This is a good place for fly fishermen as the character of the river here is not good for spin. You have to fish the channels between the rocks.

Deep in the southern part of the "Put and Take" area, the river is broad and deep. You do not see whitewater or boulders peeking above the surface at normal flow.

Flow was 241 cfs in this picture.

39.44468,-79.11142

Upstream, the river is a little tighter and features more boulders.

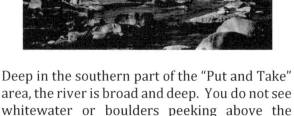

Bottom Line

Barnum is a prime fishing spot. There are plenty of fish here and plenty of people after them. The attraction of year-round, cold water is hard for the trout fisherman to resist. A sunny day brings these guys out of hibernation and into action – no matter how cold the air temperature gets!

Barnum South C&R

Summary Rating

Normal Perspective

Pressure	**Red**	Trout Size	**Green**
Physical Fitness	**Yellow**	Bass Size	**Red**
Access	**Green**	Regulations	**Green**
Hard to Find	**Green**	Stocking	**Green**
Scenery	**Green**	**Overall**	**Green**

Aggressive Perspective

Pressure	**Red**	Trout Size	**Green**
Physical Fitness	**Yellow**	Bass Size	**Red**
Access	**Red**	Regulations	**Green**
Hard to Find	**Red**	Stocking	**Green**
Scenery	**Green**	**Overall**	**Yellow**

Special Regulations

Only use artificial lures and flies. Those artificial lures must be unscented and you cannot apply scent to lures. Bait is expressly prohibited in this area.

Getting to the Stream

From the South: Navigate to Elk Garden, WV. At Elk Garden, turn north on Route 46. That road will take you past the lake; the dam and eventually intersect with Barnum Road. Turn left on Barnum Road (Co Hwy 46/2).

From the North: Navigate to Westernport, MD. Follow Route 135 west out of Westernport towards Luke. On the other side of Luke, you must turn left (south) on Route 46. Route 46 will eventually intersect with Barnum Road (Co Hwy 46/2). Turn right on Barnum Road.

There is a church at the intersection of Route 46 and Barnum Road.

Barnum Road will take you right to the river. When you hit the river, you will be in the south parking area. Visit the nice public toilets here if you have to and then follow the river upstream to reach the start of the special regulation area.

Access Point:
- Parking lot near the river (39.442391,-79.11456)

Environment and Fish

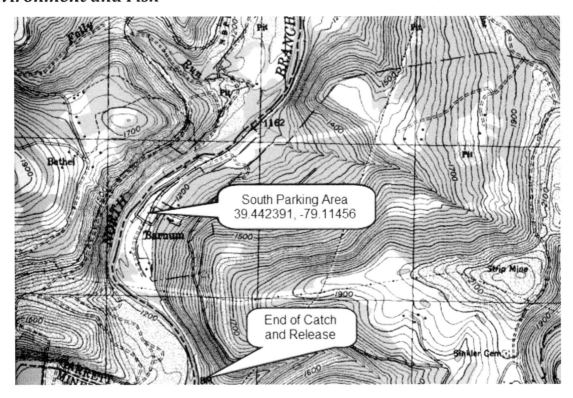

The southern catch and release area is the most popular section of the North Branch for fly fishing. Its proximity to the "off limits" stretch of the river just downstream of the dam increases the attraction as a result of the legendary large brown trout that cruise those waters. Every fall, the density of fishermen on this stretch increases dramatically as the browns migrate.

With the heavily stocked "Put and Take" section just downstream, the "catch and release, no bait" ethic seems to hold. You can walk upstream and not encounter the detritus associated with thoughtless bait fishermen. You will not see any empty bait containers or other trash scattered along the bank. This is not a fly fishing only stream, the only restrictions are fishermen release all fish and not use bait.

It's an easy walk from the southern parking lot to the river. In fact, it's almost a two-lane road leading from the lot to the large pool at the southern boundary of the catch and release area and is a key stocking point at the head of the "Put and Take" section. If you look upstream, you can see the cable and the sign marking the start of the catch and release area. Depending on whether you want to start fishing right away, you can either walk up the bank or move about 20 feet inland where there is a well-defined trail along the river. The trail becomes less distinct as you move upstream and disappears near the thicket tangle after the first bend. To pick it up again, move away from the river in a southeast direction.

Moving upstream, the river takes a hard turn to the left as the water flows down a moderate gradient to join with the initial pool. This creates an interesting spot for fishing with huge boulders and channels defining the channel. The bank on the west side is steep, forcing you to fish from the eastern shore. Since the river compresses and picks up velocity as it rolls around the curve, the current is fast under normal conditions; limiting your ability to wade at the corner. The deep water is on the west side.

Around the bend, the river becomes wadeable as it stretches wide and flat all the way up to the end of the catch and release section. There is so much water here you can fish with a number of other people and never feel pressured. You should expect to fish with many new "best friends" as a result of the popularity! Since wading is very tricky based on the current and the random, frequent deep cuts between rock formations, once you wade carefully out into the current you might find yourself working a small spot for an extended period of time. Given the density of fish in this section, that is not a bad strategy. You can have a good day on just 100 yards of this river.

The next major landmark upstream is a large island in the middle of the river at the bend. The main channel runs against the east bank with a limited, but adequate, amount of water diverted into the western channel. Both are worth fishing. Above the island, there's a broad, deep lake where a sign marks the upper boundary of the catch and release area. Fishing beyond the sign is off-limits.

Access to the river is easier downstream of the island. Approximately 50 yards downstream of the tip of the island, the bank steepens sharply; making it impossible to walk along the shore. Instead, you have to identify individual places to climb down, lurch onto rocks or wade carefully into the flow. Most of the easy spots are well marked by beaten trails from the wide path on the eastern rim that used to be a rail bed. Fishing is tough next to the eastern shore as plenty of overhanging vegetation protects the water. A better bet is to cross downstream and fish the main channel from the west.

A final point on movement is the trail you started on at the parking lot intersects the old rail bed at 39.436856,-79.113364. You can use this to move quickly up to the top of the catch and release area to claim a spot at the upper lake. In fact, if you fish this section and want to hit this pool, you should head up here early to beat the crowd. It's popular at the top spot!

Looking upstream from the entry point at the southern Barnum parking lot.

You can barely see the sign marking the start of the catch and release area at the lower middle of this picture.

This is still part of the "Put and Take" section.

View downstream from the entry point.

This pool is deep with the deepest section against the west (left) bank.

Picture taken at the bend (39.439458,-79.11684) looking downstream to the start of the catch and release section.

It's reasonably deep here but wadeable downstream of the bend. You can see the underlying rock structure in the picture.

The view upstream around the first bend.

The gradient break and associated boulders create a nice view here with a deep pool on the downstream side of each of the major boulder areas.

You have to fish this from the east bank and can wade about halfway out if the flow is moderate.

Flow was 241 cfs when I took this picture.

Upstream from the bend. It's long and flat here all the way up to the island.

You can wade with caution.

The current is fast and pushy with the slick rocks constantly challenging your ability to walk, balance and fish.

View downstream from the tip of the island vicinity 39.434768,-79.111691.

This gives you the long view and the perspective on the stretch. It is uniform in both appearance and content.

There are plenty of boulders nudging cautiously out of the river with associated deeper channels to their left or right. The deeper pools are distributed randomly in the section.

View looking south showing the downstream tip of the island in the center of the picture.

You can see the more restrained channel joining on the right with the main channel on the left.

The set of tree branches in the foreground is typical of the obstacles you will face here as a fly fisherman. If using spin gear, you can flick under these, but use a fast retrieve reel so you can get your lure in motion before the river sweeps it past your position.

The upper "lake" at 39.431635,-79.111433.

Two things to note:
- You can see the sign at the middle left of the picture that marks the old boundary
- You can see two other fishermen already working this water even though I was here early in the morning – you have to be the early bird to own that spot!

Bottom line

I don't fish this section of the North branch as often as I fish others because of the intense pressure it experiences. However, you have to acknowledge that there is a high density of fish in this section as a result of everyone's adherence to the spirit and the execution of the catch and release regulation. If you're spending a few days fishing the North Branch, you must fish this section.

Paul Sarbanes Trail

Summary Rating

Normal Perspective

Pressure	Green	Trout Size	Green
Physical Fitness	Red	Bass Size	Red
Access	Green	Regulations	Green
Hard to Find	Yellow	Stocking	Green
Scenery	Green	Overall	Green

Aggressive Perspective

Pressure	Green	Trout Size	Green
Physical Fitness	Green	Bass Size	Red
Access	Green	Regulations	Green
Hard to Find	Yellow	Stocking	Green
Scenery	Green	Overall	Green

Special Regulations

Only use artificial lures and flies. Those artificial lures must be unscented and you cannot apply scent to lures. Bait is expressly prohibited in this area.

Getting to the Stream

From the South: Navigate to Oakland, MD and head east on Route 135. Turn right on Walnut Bottom Road. It will merge with Chestnut Grove Road near the overlook. Follow Chestnut Grove Road to the right.

From the North: Navigate to Bloomington, MD and stay on Route 135 towards Oakland. Turn left onto Chestnut Grove Road and follow it to the overlook parking.

Access Point:
- Maryland Overlook 1 at the end of Chestnut Grove Road (39.440553,-79.121768)

Environment and Fish

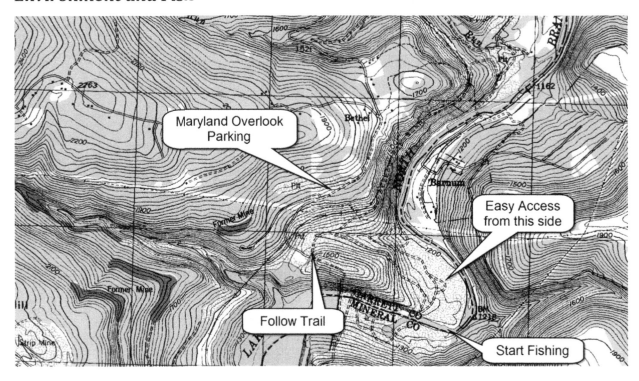

I first found out about the Paul Sarbanes trail in 2010 after publishing the first edition of this book. Thankfully, the Maryland DNR moved the upper boundary on the North Branch a few hundred yards closer to the dam to allow anglers to exploit the trail. It was not easy to find out where the trail starts with only two links being produced by an internet search as late as 2015, but eventually I decoded the puzzle and made the pilgrimage in 2012. What I discovered was a well-marked trail that requires negotiating a 500 foot vertical drop with a 1.78 mile walk to the start of fishing at the lower boundary of the protected area.

As you can see from the topographic map, the terrain is steep on the eastern shore. The bank on that side is high with limited access – especially as you approach the bend from Barnum. The western bank, on the other hand, is a broad open field that drifts down with a gradual drop in elevation to the edge of the water. Once you reach the river, the upper boundary is well marked on both the shore and the river. Be sure you do not fish to the west of those markers. Not that you need to!

After you fish near the boundary, move downriver, hit the bend and prepare to spend most of your time on the long flat stretch that terminates in the rapids at the old upper boundary. The tough hike to get here pays off with easier walking and fishing than possible from the other side. However, be aware of the long slog to get back to your vehicle and reserve enough energy! For that reason, this is a great spot to use a fishing bike.

Follow the road from the parking area down the hill.

Continue to the edge of the lake. At this point, you can fish the lake or continue to the river.

This is the trail to the river.

Follow it along the ridgeline and it will turn right into the valley.

Go through the valley and continue up and over the hill.

At the bottom, the trail breaks out into another valley on the north bank of the river.

The trail continues but you can start fishing as soon as you get beyond the off limits area marked by yellow signs on the trees next to the shore.

Paul Sarbanes Trail

Regulations and property ownership may have changed since publication.
It is your responsibility to know and obey all regulations and not trespass on private property.

51

Be sure you are downstream of this sign when you start fishing.

Yes, I know it looks great up river, but do not attempt to fish there.

The sign is at 39.431417, -79.113194.

This is the view once your go downstream around the bend.

Picture taken at 150 cfs measured on the Barnum gage.

There are deep spots, but I was able to wade comfortably. Wear a PFD and assess your ability before entering the river.

If you use the Sarbanes Trail to reach the river, you will have an easier time fishing the upper section since you can walk on the open shoreline instead of fighting the steep bank and thick trees on the other side.

Bottom Line

Simply wonderful. A tough hike leads to a wonderful stretch of the catch and release area.

Jennings Randolph Lake

Summary Rating

Normal Perspective

Pressure	**Red**	Trout Size	**Green**
Physical Fitness	**Green**	Bass Size	**Green**
Access	**Green**	Regulations	**Red**
Hard to Find	**Green**	Stocking	**Green**
Scenery	**Green**	**Overall**	**Green**

Aggressive Perspective

Pressure	**Red**	Trout Size	**Green**
Physical Fitness	**Red**	Bass Size	**Green**
Access	**Red**	Regulations	**Red**
Hard to Find	**Red**	Stocking	**Green**
Scenery	**Green**	**Overall**	**Yellow**

Special Regulations

There are no special regulations in place for the lake. You can use bait and the normal assortment of tackle.

Getting to the Stream

Maryland Boat Launch

From the South: Navigate to Oakland, MD. Follow Route 135 east from Oakland for a little over 12 miles and turn right on Mt. Zion Road. It dead-ends at the launch.

From the North: Navigate to Westernport, MD. Take Route 135 west out of Westernport towards Luke and follow it across the Savage River in Bloomington. You will be on Route 135 for a little over 8 miles and then turn left onto Mt. Zion Road. It dead-ends at the launch.

Here is the Army Corps of Engineering's description of the Maryland Boat Launch: *"The Maryland Boat Launch is on Mt. Zion Road off Maryland State route 135 on Backbone Mountain. The launch includes a thirty-foot wide, 600-foot long concrete boat ramp with a floating pier system. The large paved parking area can accommodate fifty cars and trailers and a comfort facility is available for the boater's convenience. Both the comfort station and the launch ramp are lighted at night. The Maryland service charge will be $5.00 for launching a boat."*

Jennings Randolph Lake   Regulations and property ownership may have changed since publication.   53

It is your responsibility to know and obey all regulations and not trespass on private property.

West Virginia (Howell Run) Boat Launch

From the South: Navigate to Elk Garden, WV. At Elk Garden, turn north on Route 46. That road will take you to the lake. Turn left at the sign for the Howell Boat Launch. If you get to the turn for the overlook, you have gone too far.

From the North: Navigate to Westernport, MD. Follow Route 135 west out of Westernport towards Luke. On the other side of Luke, you must turn left (south) on Route 46. Turn right at the sign for the Howell Boat Launch. You will go past the turn for the overlook and beach – the turn to the Howell Launch is farther south. As of 2014, there is no fee to use it.

Here is the Army Corps of Engineering's description of the Howell Run Boat Launch: *"The Howell Run Boat Launch (located off WV State Route 46) consists of a wide two-lane concrete ramp, with a floating dock for temporary loading and unloading of boats. The large paved parking area ensures plenty of parking spaces and a comfort facility is available for the boater's convenience. A vault toilet comfort station is available at the launch facility. Both the comfort station and the launch ramp are lighted at night."*

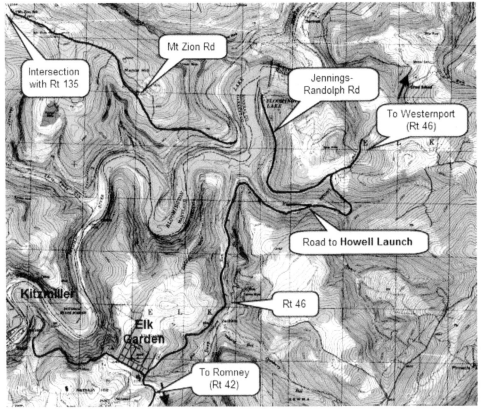

You can get up-to-date information on the lake conditions, local weather forecast and other pertinent lake related information by calling 304-355-2890. Remember when you drive to the Howell Launch, most of the signs will focus on the overlook at the end of Jennings-Randolph Road. Do not turn at the major turn that marks the intersection of Jennings-Randolph with Route 46. Instead, find the small, nondescript (but marked) turn to the launch south of the Overlook turn.

Access Points:

- Maryland Boat Launch (39.419685,-79.12993)
- West Virginia Howell Run Boat Launch (39.409556,-79.12008)

Environment and Fish

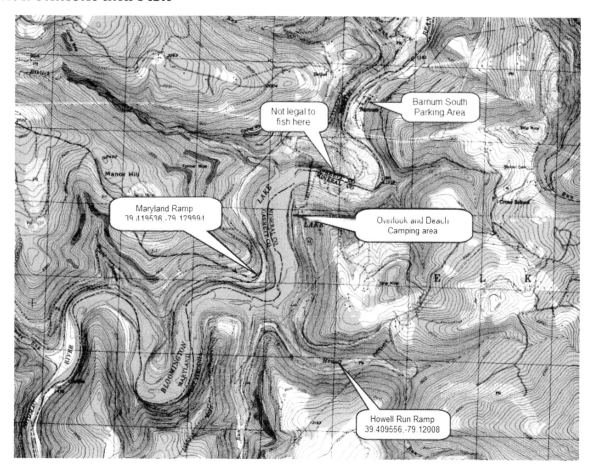

It's time for a full disclosure. I do not have a bass boat. I have a canoe -- a small canoe. Bringing a canoe to a lake this large is like bringing a knife to a gunfight; you are probably going to come out on the short end of the stick. That certainly was the case the one time I finished Jennings-Randolph Lake.

This is a lake where you really do need the proper equipment to exploit the vibrant fish population that exists here. In fact, monsters lurk in the depths with a 14 pound walleye caught in 1998. The first challenge is just getting from point to point. From talking to other fishermen, the best spot for smallmouth is up at the mouth of the lake leading to Kitzmiller. Running five or six miles up the lake is not a big deal in a high powered bass boat that can go fast enough to make your cheeks flap, but it's a heck of a challenge in a canoe pushed by paddles or, at best, a trolling motor. You could spend an hour or more just getting across this huge body of water.

But, that's exactly what I did… or tried to do. I cranked the trolling motor into what it calls "high" and started grinding my way up the lake in a desperate attempt to reach perfect smallmouth water. I did stop and fish a little bit along the shoreline but was repeatedly battered by huge waves kicked off by ski boats, skidoos and bass boats as they churned across the lake. Not that they were doing anything wrong, it's just that a huge wave can flip a canoe if it is pointed in the wrong direction. I found I had to repeatedly reorient the boat to point the bow into the wave to avoid taking the full force on the side of the canoe; something that would have flipped me over.

Eventually, common sense got the better of me and I gave up and headed back to the launch.

It is impossible to fish the lake from the shoreline in the upper section because there is no shoreline to walk on. As you can see from the map sheet, the lake is in a deep, steep valley. The closeness of the contour lines on the map provides a dramatic indication of how steep the shoreline is. If you were to try and walk the shoreline, you would always feel like you are about to tip over and roll downhill.

Once out on the water, chances are no matter where you are in the lake, there are tens if not hundreds of feet of water below your boat as the depths here range all the way up to 270 feet. This makes fishing problematic. You can bounce jigs and Texas rigged plastics down the steep shoreline or you can troll for walleye in the deeper water. Until you get into the upper reaches of the lake where the gradient gradually slopes up to the spot where the river joins the lake, all you are going to find is deep, dark water.

Howell Boat Launch

Mt Zion (MD) Boat Launch

View down towards the head of the dam.

You can begin to get a sense of the size of the lake from this picture. It was taken near the entrance to the cove that contains the Howell Run boat launch.

39.415309,-79.128213

Looking south from 39.416104,-79.140959 at the entry to the finger of the lake that leads up to Kitzmiller.

Looking west from 39.416088,-79.150422.

There is a nice stream coming in at the right of the picture -- it's a pretty good spot.

Bottom Line

Leave this to the folks with boats.

Kitzmiller

Summary Rating

Normal Perspective

Pressure	Green	Trout Size	Yellow
Physical Fitness	Red	Bass Size	Yellow
Access	Red	Regulations	Red
Hard to Find	Green	Stocking	Green
Scenery	Green	**Overall**	Yellow

Aggressive Perspective

Pressure	Green	Trout Size	Yellow
Physical Fitness	Green	Bass Size	Yellow
Access	Green	Regulations	Red
Hard to Find	Red	Stocking	Green
Scenery	Green	**Overall**	Yellow

Special Regulations

None – this is 6 miles of "Put and Take" water from the southern end of Jennings-Randolph Lake to the boundary of the Potomac State Forest a few miles upstream from Kitzmiller.

Getting to the Stream

Navigate to Kitzmiller, MD and locate East Main Street (39.392494,-79.180398). East Main Street is the first right north of the river and runs next to west bank of the river. As you drive up East Main, you will see the reassuring "Stocked Water" signs next to the river.

Go to the dead end at north end of East Main and park in a small pull-off on the right. Please do not park on the yard of the house on the other side of the street.

Access Points:
- North end of East Main Street (39.392494,-79.180398)
- Park on the east side of the railroad tracks in West Virginia (39.386474,-79.180462)
- Park on the Maryland side of the bridge in Kitzmiller (39.387436,-79.181492)
- Park at the school at the end of West Main Street (39.387353,-79.189003)
- Intersection of Shalimar and North Hill Road (39.38934,-79.194626)
- Various other turnouts along Shalimar - the last one is at the confluence of Abram Creek (39.379682,-79.202455)

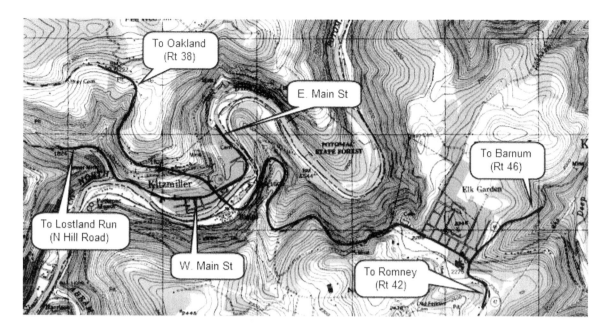

While East Main leads to the parking area that is the jump off into the eastern portion of the Kitzmiller "Put and Take" area, you can follow West Main to move farther upstream and access the river from Shalimar Road.

Be sure you stay to the left at the "Y" intersection where Shalimar joins North Hill Road. The good section of the upstream "Put and Take" section begins at the "Y" (39.389161,-79.194324).

There are several deep, wide pools at the intersection, so you may as well start fishing right there if you intend to hit the upstream area from Kitzmiller. There are a number of places you can pull off and, with a short slide into the river, fish directly from the road.

Downstream

Environment and Fish

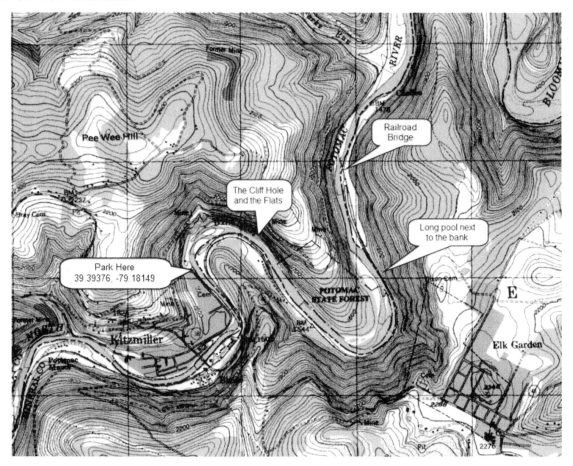

Kitzmiller is the first place on the North Branch above Westernport to provide an opportunity to fish for both smallmouth bass and trout. In itself, that presents a significant dilemma. Depending on how far you want to walk, you'll move from one species to the next.

The lake formed by Jennings-Randolph Dam is approximately 4 1/2 miles downstream from where you park at the end of East Main Street. It supports a vibrant population of smallmouth bass that were first stocked in the lake in the mid-90s. The closer you get to the lake, the closer you get to a higher population of smallmouth. On the other hand, the stocked trout will cluster closer to the city since that is where they are stocked. While the DNR map depicts the stocked area vicinity of Kitzmiller as extending downstream all the way to the railroad bridge, the Maryland Western Region fisheries office confirmed that the DNR only stocks off the road – not from the rail bed as they do in the delayed harvest area.

This limitation means trout penetration into the downstream area depends on the natural migration that will occur once trout are stocked up in Kitzmiller. There are a number of studies, to include a

Pennsylvania study, which demonstrated stocked trout only hold in place for a small number of days and then start to migrate downstream. Depending on the nature of the water, they could move as much as 700 yards with some fish going for miles. Based on that, you can expect to find trout during stocking season within a reasonable distance of Kitzmiller. But, if you want to pursue both species of fish, you are better off moving farther downstream and then fishing your way back up.

You need a wading staff as this is the North Branch and it features all the slippery rocks you expect in this river. If you fish your way back to Kitzmiller, you need to be in decent physical condition since you will have to lurch from rock to rock with every step. There are no trails along the banks.

I know I am using the words "scenic" and "beautiful" far too much in this Book. Fortunately, those words describe much of the North Branch and Kitzmiller, once you are away from the town, is no exception.

As you transition upstream from the wide inlet formed by the Jennings-Randolph Lake, the river quickly tightens up as it begins to run through a deep canyon extending most of the way back to Kitzmiller. The only way to get into this section is to either float the river or walk next to the rail bed; being careful to avoid trespassing on railroad property. In fact, be alert for any "No Trespassing" signs that may have been posted. The railroad bridge is the key landmark. It is approximately 2.5 miles downstream of the town and marks the spot where the character of the river transitions from lake to wild. From the bridge upstream, it's typically 50 to 60 feet across with plenty of rocks and fallen tree structure to absorb your attention and shelter the fish.

The river maintains that perspective until you round the major bend looping south towards Elk Garden. Near 39.38926, -79.16843, there's a small valley that allows the river to flatten out and create a uniformly shallow (1 to 2 feet) section dominated by flat water with numerous rocks nudging above the surface. On the northern side, there is a narrow plateau you can use to leave the river and move quickly upstream. The few hunting stands perched in the trees in this area mark the downstream penetration of evidence of other humans. Likewise, you can leave the river on the southern bank in this section, but you have to stumble across rocks as opposed to the smoother ground near the hunting stands. Clearly, this is not the place to be in the fall during hunting season. If you fish late in the year, wear blaze orange.

A cliff face appears on the north bank of the river sheltering a nice deep hole washed in the last fast water prior to slowing into the broader downstream valley. A short distance upstream is a moderate gradient break where the river careens around the sharp bend just downstream of the town. The bend features a good deep section that is perfect trout water.

Looking upstream to the bridge (back towards Kitzmiller).

This is the railroad bridge about 2.5 miles down from Kitzmiller.

Flow running at 242 cfs

Downstream from the bridge (towards the lake).

You can see the river start to flatten out as it transitions into the inlet to Jennings Randolph Lake.

The water level in the lake dictates where the final transition occurs.

If you are after smallies, this section is good.

As you fish your way upstream, the river adopts a consistent geography. There will be gradient driven rapids followed by calm spots such as this.

Smallies cling to the shady areas where there is deeper water.

The center of the river in these areas is typically two feet deep and you can wade up the middle and pepper both banks with casts.

62   Regulations and property ownership may have changed since publication.   Kitzmiller

It is your responsibility to know and obey all regulations and not trespass on private property.

Picture vicinity 39.397005,-79.16585 from the top of a typical gradient break looking back to the bend in the river upstream from the railroad bridge.

Plenty of great structure here to fish. Each of the rocks in this picture shelters a good holding pool.

Many of these offered up nice 12" smallies.

At regular intervals, the river pours over a break to spill to a lower level.

All of these breaks oxygenate the water and attract fish.

At the top of this picture, there is a wide lake area bordering the track (39.394551,-79.164176). If you do not want to walk the entire 2.5 miles from Kitzmiller to the bridge, this is the first good spot to enter the river.

You should walk to the northern end where the track dives back into the woods and start fishing upstream. From that spot, if you follow the river downstream another 50 yards, you will stand here. Right behind you is a great spot where a downed tree shelters some deep, fast water.

The left bank of the river is deep here.

You can see the downed tree mentioned in the previous picture.

This is the downstream end of the "Kitzmiller Flats."

If you decide it is too shallow to be worthwhile, you can skip it and move up to the cliff face shown in the next picture.

The lower section of the Flats is easy to negotiate. If you want to move fast, you can leave the water on the right hand bank and walk through the woods. There is a trail, of sorts, you can follow.   You will have to bushwhack through some tall, thick bushes to return to the stream.

This is the cliff pool just downstream of the large bend by Kitzmiller.

Approach this carefully and you will pick up some fish here.

The junction where the "B" in "Branch" is on the map (39.396855,-79.177287).

The river takes a sharp downhill run.

Fish the end of the rapids where it empties into the flats.

This nice spot is just around the corner from where you will park at the end of East Main.

It is tough to fish from the right hand bank. Cross to the other side to get a good angle.

It is very deep on the right hand side with plenty of good rocks and boulders under the surface providing holding structure.

Bottom Line:

I did not see anyone else, or evidence of anyone else, once I got about 1/2 mile downstream of Kitzmiller. There are fish here. You should take your smallie flies and tackle with you and focus on smallies until you approach within a reasonable distance of Kitzmiller where you should switch patterns in the hope of finding some of those stocked fish.

There is not much hope for any holdover trout given that this part of the North Branch periodically blows through 80 degrees in the summer. This is a place where you need to bring a decent lunch so you can perch on a rock and savor the sun while listening to the roar of the river.

Be alert for any changes in property ownership. Even though a section of a stream falls within the stocked area, it does not necessarily mean that it is open to the public. Given so much fishable water across the state, the DNR cannot keep up with the vagaries of individual landowner desires. Rest assured that when private property restrictions become excessive, that location will drop from the stocking plan. Therefore, anything stocked should have reasonable public access. Pay close attention to the posted signs and respect private property; do not trespass.

Kitzmiller

Regulations and property ownership may have changed since publication.
It is your responsibility to know and obey all regulations and not trespass on private property.

65

Upstream

Environment and Fish

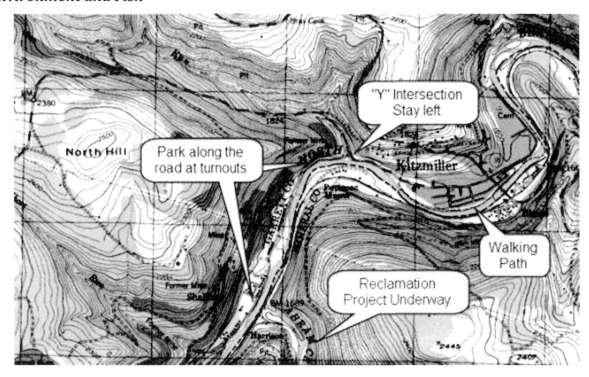

You are not limited to fishing downstream from Kitzmiller; the "Put and Take" section extends several miles upstream to the boundary of the Potomac State Forest. In addition to the parking area at the end of East Main St. discussed above, there are plenty of options for parking and access to the upstream stretch.

- Park on the east side of the railroad tracks in West Virginia (39.386474,-79.180462)
- Park on the Maryland side of the bridge in Kitzmiller (39.387436,-79.181492)
- Park at the school at the end of W. Main St. (39.387353,-79.189003)
- Park at the junction of N. Hill Rd. and Shalimar road
- Park anywhere along Shalimar road where you can pull off and walk to the river

Parking near the bridge gives you access to the broad, shallow section near the town of Kitzmiller. If you want to move upstream quickly to survey your options for attacking this part of the river, I recommend you cross to the Maryland side and walk up the asphalt sidewalk along the river -- no need to stumble across rocks if you're just looking.

Bordering the town, the deeper water exists on the West Virginia bank and is easily accessible from the Maryland side. The water improves at the intersection of N. Hill Rd. and Shalimar where there is a series of dramatic, deep pools near the bend in the river. On a typical day, you can see people perched on the banks plumbing the depths -- mostly using bait. To fish this stretch, you should park at the school at the end of W. Main St. and work your way up the river to the pools. There are some small turnouts just beyond the intersection that can hold one or two trucks. Before you leave, fish the boundary of the gradient break entering the pools as well as upstream where the river tightens before turning south.

Once you round the bend and head south on Shalimar Rd., the river returns to being broad and flat. The next 3/4 mile is similar to the section by the cliff hole encountered fishing downstream from Kitzmiller. There are plenty of large rocks and boulders to create pools holding fish. You can wade, but be prepared to encounter deep cuts in random locations.

The next major landmark is the intersection of Abram Creek with the North Branch. There is a deep pool on the main stem of the river at the junction that deserves your attention. Abram is listed as troubled water as a result of high concentrations of metals and acid left over from mining activity and will not support trout. In 2008, West Virginia began a reclamation project to remediate the Creek using lime sand and dosers. Given the success of this technology throughout West Virginia, you should expect to see the return of trout to Abrams Creek in the coming years.

Just upstream of the junction, Shalimar Road dead ends into private property marked by a gate and a sign to asking you to keep out.

As a general comment, there are no "stocked trout water" signs along the Shalimar Road. The Maryland DNR assured me that there is public access to this stretch of water as long as you do not encounter a posted sign. Clearly, the removal of those signs was an initiative by the local population to limit pressure. Ignore that and feel free to fish here as long as you do not violate private property.

Picture taken looking upstream from the school at the end of West Main Street (39.387105,-79.189271)

Flow was 212 cfs at the Kitzmiller gage

Kitzmiller

Regulations and property ownership may have changed since publication.
It is your responsibility to know and obey all regulations and not trespass on private property.

67

View upstream from the junction of Shalimar Road and North Hill Road.

All of these pools deserve attention

View downstream from the junction of Shalimar Road and North Hill Road.

This becomes a swimming hole in the summer.

Picture taken farther upstream at the end of the pool section.

Climb down and fish the head of the pool. There are some small runs in this section, but it would be better to park on the upstream end where you can also fish the "flats".

This is the junction of Abram Creek and the North Branch (39.379136,-79.201952). There is a deep pool to the left of this picture that gets plenty of attention.

View downstream into the flats section from Abram Creek.

There is plenty of structure to hold both fish and your attention.

Bottom Line

If you enjoy the "Put and Take" area at Barnum, you will enjoy this section as well. The access is simple with no steep banks to negotiate. The key difference is that once you move beyond the intersection, there are no deep, single pools until you get to the junction of Abram Creek. This makes using spin gear a challenge in fast water.

Kitzmiller
Regulations and property ownership may have changed since publication.
It is your responsibility to know and obey all regulations and not trespass on private property.
69

Lostland Run

Summary Rating

Normal Perspective

Pressure	Green	Trout Size	Green
Physical Fitness	Red	Bass Size	Yellow
Access	Yellow	Regulations	Yellow
Hard to Find	Yellow	Stocking	Green
Scenery	Green	**Overall**	Green

Aggressive Perspective

Pressure	Green	Trout Size	Green
Physical Fitness	Green	Bass Size	Yellow
Access	Yellow	Regulations	Yellow
Hard to Find	Yellow	Stocking	Green
Scenery	Green	**Overall**	Green

Special Regulations

Lostland Run is the first access point in the Delayed Harvest area. The boundary begins downstream at the border of the Potomac State Forest and ends at the upstream boundary of the forest near Steyer.

From the DNR regulations: *"From June 16 through September 30, the daily creel limit and possession limit is two trout (all species of trout in aggregate). During this period no special bait, lure or tackle restrictions are in effect. From October 1 through June 15, a person may not keep or have any trout in possession while fishing in these areas.*

A person may fish only with artificial lures, including artificial flies and streamers. The use or possession of any natural bait, bait fish, fish bait, scents or natural or synthetic devices capable of catching fish other than artificial lures is prohibited."

Lostland Run is a place where you can actually get away from the "maddening crowd" and hike for a long way without running into a road. The next access point up river from Lostland is Laurel Run; 2.85 miles upstream.

Access Point:
- Lostland Run parking lot (39.362888,-79.23275)

Getting to the Stream

From the east: When you come into Kitzmiller from West Virginia on Route 42, turn left onto West Main Street once you cross the bridge. West Main eventually becomes Shalimar Road. Follow it past the school and be alert for North Hill Road. It will veer off to the right.

Turn onto North Hill Road and follow it until it dead-ends. At the stop sign, turn left onto Potomac Camp Road. After approximately 1.7 miles, be alert for a small bridge.

Turn left on the dirt road immediately after the bridge (39.381814,-79.277773) shown in this picture.

From the west: Heading southeast out of Oakland on Route 135, turn right onto Route 560. Follow it and turn left on Bethlehem Road. Bethlehem will come to a "Y" intersection. Stay on Bethlehem Road by taking the right branch of the "Y". Turn left onto Combination Road and then another left on Potomac Camp Road.

After a mile, you will see the dirt road on your right (pictured) that leads to Lostland Run.

If you cross the bridge shown, you just missed the turn (39.381814,-79.277773).

You will pass the headquarters for the Potomac State Forest on your left before you come to this turn. Heads up!

Follow the dirt road all the way to the end - it will seem like it never ends and you will become anxious as you are probably desperate to both fish and get out of the truck after the long drive. There are deep ruts in the dirt road depending on the maintenance level, but you can get over them in a normal car if you are careful.

Park at the trailhead (39.362888,-79.23275) and look for the dim trail to the river at the entrance to the parking area (you drove past it to enter the parking lot). If you go down the well-marked, obvious trail leading from the parking lot at the far end, you will end up at the swimming holes – they are fishable if you beat the swimmers.

Lostland Run

Regulations and property ownership may have changed since publication.
It is your responsibility to know and obey all regulations and not trespass on private property.

71

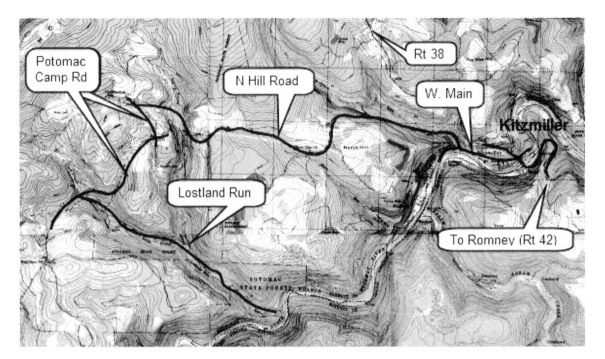

There are 6 roadside camping spaces off of Lostland Run road. Reservation required. You can reserve a site by calling 301-334-2038.

Register and pay the fee at the kiosk at the head of Lostland Run.

Fill out one of the forms in the container hanging from the kiosk and put the form and the fee in the slot of the pipe on the right.

You get a good look at one of the lime dosers on the right as you head down the road to the trailhead.

The river owes its recovery to these machines and the vision of the folks who worked the bureaucracy successfully to get them installed.

There are 4 total dosers in the North Branch complex constantly feeding lime into the water to neutralize the acid.

If you look just downstream of the doser, you can see how the lime coats the stream, allowing the water to pick up the buffering chemical

There is a public restroom just beyond the doser. Low clearance vehicles need to exercise care as they get closer to the trailhead. While the road is good up near all the campsites, it gets rough near the river. Watch your speed and you will not scrape bottom.

Mile 1

Environment and Fish

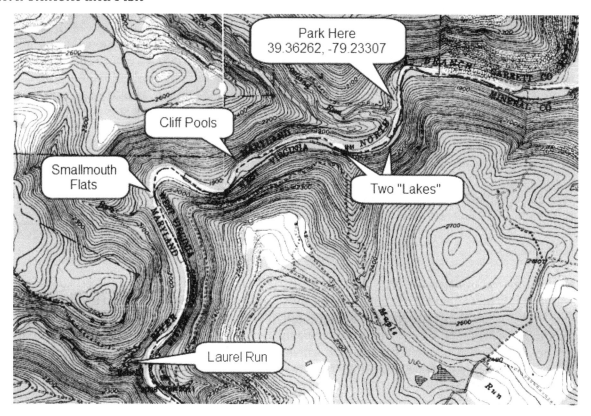

The North Branch at Lostland Run has the appearance of a tight western mountain stream; looking and smelling like the McCloud River in California. As such, it presents a stark contrast to the river you encountered in either Kitzmiller or downstream in the Barnum section.

The rail bed is active and you should not walk on it.

All railroad property is automatically posted, no signs required, in both West Virginia and Maryland.

Your first challenge upon bursting through the undergrowth that separates the river from the parking area is to decide which bank you are going to fish from. In higher water conditions, it becomes very tough to work up the right-hand (north) bank as the brush pushes tight against the river and does not give you any room to maneuver. You are forced to clamber over rocks and boulders as you move from place to place.

This initial section of the river is mostly fast-moving water plunging around large boulders and slippery cuts. Whether you fish with a fly or spin rod, it is a productive area to focus on - but you must be on the right hand bank if the water is high. Of the two methods of fishing, you can pick up trout easier with fly gear rigged for nymphs. Your spinner will get swept away quickly and have limited time to start its action. If you are a spin guy, you may want to get some nymphs and rig them under a small slip bobber using light tackle.

At the first major bend upstream, you encounter a wide stretch with a deep pool that cannot be waded in high water. The deepest section is towards the south bank of the river and you can fish it if you approach carefully from the middle of the river. Once you penetrate as far as you can, skip around to the head of the pool and work in from there. Above the pool, there's a high gradient/run area about 70 yards long. The lower 25 yards is the best place as it features the deeper runs and cuts that will hold most of the fish.

Continuing upstream, you encounter the first true "lake" in this section. It's a broad oval body of water that is unwadeable from much of the shore. It drops off from the bank steeply on the left-hand side and closes out on the right. This lake is full of both trout (in season) and smallmouth bass. You should work around both sides of it - particularly the right-hand side up against the bank where there are boulders and overhanging trees. You will not be able to penetrate very far on the right-hand side because it quickly closes out against the steeply pitched mountain now forming the right-hand boundary of the river

Once you finish the tail and left bank, walk up to the head of the lake and fish the narrow channel. You will catch a number of trout and smallies actively feeding in the current seams marked by the bubble line.

At this point, the northern bank is totally closed out. Your only option to move upstream is on the southern bank. Luckily, it's fairly easy to walk near the stream as the bank is a wide, mildly slanting hill. You will have to bushwhack through some vegetation to move from place to place. Be sure you tuck your trousers into your socks or you will end up with a few ticks.

The two best holes in this section of the river are above the oval lake and are about a mile away from the trailhead. They are tight against a cliff face and will be obvious when you see them. I'm not giving away any secrets as these spots are obvious "gold" places.

In the lower pool below the cliff face, there is a rock shelf you may not be able to see if the water is high. That shelf separates the pool into two sections. Be sure and throw your nymphs or streamers beyond that shelf into the seam beyond it. It's deep there and the fish hold near the bottom. For the spin guys, this is another place to use a slip bobber.

Looking upstream from the trailhead on a high flow day (359 cfs) in July.

You can get an appreciation for the tough walking here by looking at the jumble of rocks.

You have to climb over the boulder on the right.

The same section as above, looking downstream on a high flow day with the water running at 359 cfs.

Plenty of big boulders provide shelter and holding areas.

This is the wide pool.

As you can see, the left hand bank looks great with the overhanging trees.

You will not be able to wade all the way through it if the water is at normal levels.

Pretty trout being released – remember you must release all trout during the delayed harvest season!

This is the first lake, the wide oval section with a view at the tight channel feeding its head.

You can fish from the left hand shore all the way around it, but you will not be able to wade very far into it.

You need a sink tip line to really work this over. The right hand side (not shown) has great vegetation and deep sections.

This is the lower pool at the cliff.

You can barely see the submerged rock shelf in the lower center of this picture.

You need to throw to the other side and float your lure in the seam at the edge of the current.

Bottom line

Mile 1 of Lostland Run is prime fishing country. Since you can walk away from the trailhead and still be on great water, you rarely encounter a crowd here. In all the times I fished this section, I have only seen a few other fishermen.

If you only have one place to fish in the delayed harvest area, it should be this spot.

Mile 2

Environment and Fish

Starting at the cliff hole discussed in the Mile One section, there is a fast transition in the character of the river. In the first mile, it's mostly tight runs compressing the flow and making it difficult to move from bank to bank while the upper section runs through a wider, low gradient valley that allows the water to spread out and slow down. The railroad tracks continue to hug the river on the left (eastern) bank forming a high ridge that slopes down an easy grade to the river. The water is generally shallow here, ranging in depth from 1 to 2 feet with deeper areas where the water has cut a gash in the riverbed. Of course, the depth will depend on the flow, so pay attention to the gage.

There are no pristine pools. There are no oval lakes, cliff pools or similar areas to provide obvious targets. However, there are plenty of fish. You need to exercise your normal stream craft skills to find them. In particular, this area is full of smallmouth bass ranging up to 12 inches in size. They huddle behind the rocks and consistently fall victim to surface attacks. During the height of trout stocking season, there are decent numbers of trout in this area as well, but the shallow water subjects them to increased predation. As a result of their hatchery fresh, silvery color, they are more likely to fall victim to the natural predators that thrive in the Potomac State Forest. Over time their color changes to match their wild cousins, but it may take a few months.

If you are a spin fisherman, this section of the river is challenging because it is shallow. You may find yourself constantly becoming hung up as your spinner bounces across the bottom. The deeper cuts in the riverbed are tight, deep and do not allow a spinner to achieve its full action at the appropriate depth. If you fish in this section, I recommend you stick with a fly presentation. As noted above, either dry flies or nymphs will work.

This picture looks upstream into Mile Two.

I call this the "smallmouth flats" section of the river as a result of the vibrant population I found here (39.35524, -79.25674)

Note how shallow the water is – you can see the bottom in these pictures.

This is the cliff hole mentioned in the Mile One section.

It has a deep long run parallel to the bank next to the cliff. You can work it from the left bank or float a nymph down from the head of the pool.

The water is crystal clear, approach carefully!

Typical North Branch smallie. These guys are not big, but they are all smallie and put up a heck of a fight.

You should target the various rocks poking above the surface. The smallies lie in wait in front or in back.

Terrestrials, attractors, poppers and streamers are good to land these guys.

Looking upstream towards Laurel Run.

It is around the far corner.

You can see that the river becomes even shallower here.

Work nymphs around the rocks where you find adequate depth.

Bottom Line

While Mile Two is not as good as Mile One, it is a fantastic stretch protected by the long walk to get here. Granted, you can walk downstream from Laurel Run to work into the upper portion, but it is at least a mile walk from that trailhead to get to the smallmouth flats.

Laurel Run

Summary Rating

Normal Perspective

Pressure	**Red**	Trout Size	**Green**
Physical Fitness	**Yellow**	Bass Size	**Yellow**
Access	**Red**	Regulations	**Yellow**
Hard to Find	**Red**	Stocking	**Green**
Scenery	**Green**	**Overall**	**Yellow**

Aggressive Perspective

Pressure	**Red**	Trout Size	**Green**
Physical Fitness	**Yellow**	Bass Size	**Yellow**
Access	**Green**	Regulations	**Yellow**
Hard to Find	**Green**	Stocking	**Green**
Scenery	**Green**	**Overall**	**Yellow**

Special Regulations

This is in the Delayed Harvest area. The boundary begins downstream of the access point at the border of the Potomac State Forest and ends at the upstream boundary of the forest near Steyer.

From the DNR regulations: *"From June 16 through September 30, the daily creel limit and possession limit is two trout (all species of trout in aggregate). During this period no special bait, lure or tackle restrictions are in effect. From October 1 through June 15, a person may not keep or have any trout in possession while fishing in these areas.*

A person may fish only with artificial lures, including artificial flies and streamers. The use or possession of any natural bait, bait fish, fish bait, scents or natural or synthetic devices capable of catching fish other than artificial lures is prohibited."

Getting to the Stream

From Oakland: Head south on Route 560 from Oakland. Do not turn at the sign for Potomac State Forest; continue south. Be alert for the turn to the east onto White Church Road.

From Gormania: In Gormania, Route 560 is the main road on the Maryland side of the river. Head north from Gormania on Route 560. Be alert for the turn to the east onto White Church Road.

Once on White Church, be alert for the place where the road takes a hard right.

There is a small, brown sign for the State Forest at a sharp bend (see map below). Instead of charging around the bend to the right, slow down and go straight (39.337617,-79.309831). This puts you onto a small road (Audley Riley Road) that turns to gravel. Follow it until you see a large brown forest service sign. It will point you to Wallman on the right and to Laurel Run on the left. This is also where you can self-register for one of the camping spots. Stay left to go to Laurel Run. Follow the road - it's a long haul - past a number of nice camping spots. You cannot make a wrong turn. Eventually, the road will dead end. The road is pretty rough once you go beyond the bridge. You will not need a 4x4, but you will have to be careful you do not scrape.

At the end of the road, gear up and walk across Laurel Run onto the grassy trail that would have been the logical continuation of the road if the rock wall was not present.

You can see the trail/road on the other side of the stream.

Park to the left of the rock wall to allow other folks space to turn around.

Follow the road for 100 yards beyond the stream and it will dump you onto the river.

Access Point:
- Laurel Run parking lot (39.34344,-79.25987)

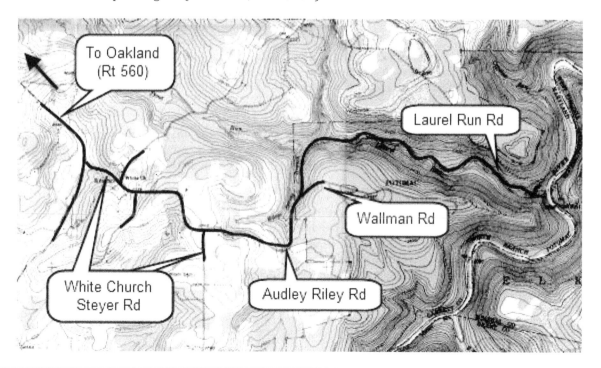

Environment and Fish

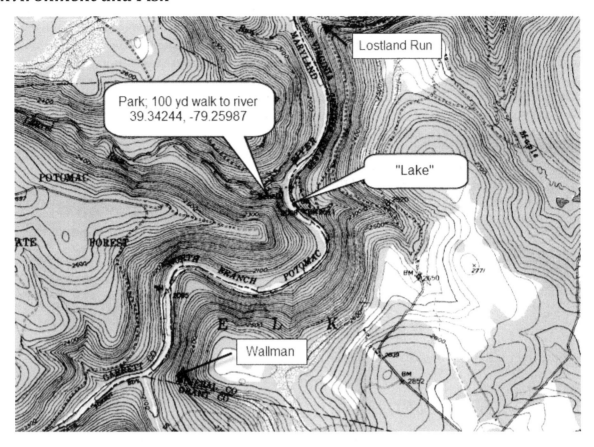

I have not seen much written about Laurel Run - most discussion related to the delayed harvest area centers on the Lostland Run and Wallman access points. After visiting this spot, I can understand why. First, the North Branch is the North Branch. The river features the same cascading rocky runs with the pools you expect. The joy and the issue is that there is a large "lake" about 40 yards to the south of where the access trail hits the river.

The lake looks like it provides a nice swimming hole as well as a fishing site. The quantity of beer cans indicates a party destination - so if you are expecting a nice day on the river, I recommend you go someplace else - or come here when the weather is not good for swimming. I checked on www.swimmingholes.org to confirm my suspicions.

If you do go here, I recommend you walk south, past the lake and cross the river where you can. As you hike farther south, the human pressure drops - no additional dense trash - and the fishing improves. Eventually, you will run into Wallman North. Although it would be a shorter walk to get to the lower end of Wallman North by walking south from Laurel, it is an easier walk north from Wallman if the water is high. The west river bank at Laurel is very tough going. It is high and steep where any misstep will send you spilling onto the rocks below. There is a small trail that appears and disappears, but it will have you crawling over rocks for most of the way. Eventually, you break out on a small knoll overlooking a lake area.

Your goal needs to be to get to the other side of the river at the first place you can find a safe crossing. It will be definitely easier to fish the lake from that side (assuming it is not being used for swimming). In terms of

82   Regulations and property ownership may have changed since publication.   Laurel Run

It is your responsibility to know and obey all regulations and not trespass on private property.

fishing, this section features spot pools; pools formed in eddies behind the bigger rocks. These hold fish and you can catch both smallies and trout. Other than the lake, there are no large pools in the immediate vicinity of the trailhead. I find most pools are overfished and you can do better working the larger rocks in the stream. Any place with a section of calm water created by a large rock should hold a fish or two.

View upstream from where the trail hits the river with the Steyer Gage reading 86 cfs.

The large lake (aka swimming hole) is at the top of this picture.

If you continue up the right hand side of the river, the going will be tough. The trail comes and goes. You weave between tightly spaced trees and must balance on a skinny path.

Trail to the river.

On your TOPO map, this will show as a road. You cannot drive on it.

The road dead ends where the road crosses Laurel Run. Park there and walk - it's only 100 yards.

This shot is looking downstream at the lower part of the "lake".

The old bridge is where you hit the river on the trail and it is worth fishing downstream a bit from it as well as in the small pools nearby.

Bottom Line

It's scenic and pretty and the series of pools below the railroad bridge are nice. The farther upstream into the Wallman section you get, the better the water becomes.

Wallman

Summary Rating

Normal Perspective

Pressure	**Green**	Trout Size	**Green**
Physical Fitness	**Green**	Bass Size	**Yellow**
Access	**Yellow**	Regulations	**Yellow**
Hard to Find	**Red**	Stocking	**Green**
Scenery	**Green**	**Overall**	**Green**

Aggressive Perspective

Pressure	**Green**	Trout Size	**Green**
Physical Fitness	**Red**	Bass Size	**Yellow**
Access	**Yellow**	Regulations	**Yellow**
Hard to Find	**Green**	Stocking	**Green**
Scenery	**Green**	**Overall**	**Green**

Special Regulations

Wallman is the last section of the Delayed Harvest area. The border of the Potomac State Forest is just upstream of the southern parking lot.

"From June 16 through September 30, the daily creel limit and possession limit is two trout (all species of trout in aggregate). During this period no special bait, lure or tackle restrictions are in effect. From October 1 through June 15, a person may not keep or have any trout in possession while fishing in these areas.

A person may fish only with artificial lures, including artificial flies and streamers. The use or possession of any natural bait, bait fish, fish bait, scents or natural or synthetic devices capable of catching fish other than artificial lures is prohibited."

Access Points:
- Wallman north parking lot (39.32230,-79.28346)
- Wallman middle parking lot (39.31453,-79.28459)
- Wallman south parking lot (39.30861,-79.28636)

Getting to the Stream

From Oakland: Head south on Route 560 from Oakland. Do not turn at the sign for Potomac State Forest; continue south. Be alert for the turn to the east onto White Church Road.

From Gormania: In Gormania, Route 560 is the main road on the Maryland side of the river. Head north from Gormania on Route 560. Be alert for the turn to the east onto White Church Road.

Once on White Church, be alert for the place where the road takes a hard right. There is a small, brown sign for the State Forest at the sharp bend (see map below). Instead of charging around the bend to the right, slow down and go straight (39.337617,-79.309831). This puts you onto a small road (Audley Riley Road) that turns to gravel. Follow it until you see a large brown forest service sign. It will point you to Wallman on the right and to Laurel Run on the left. This is also where you can self-register for one of the camping spots.

Stay right to go to Wallman and head up the hill. There is a public restroom on the left just beyond the top of the hill.

At the next Y intersection (marked by a sign that says "State Forest Parking"), veer right and continue to follow the gravel road. It takes you down the side of the mountain, and the road is usually well maintained. You do not normally need a high clearance vehicle.

Ignore the small dirt road on the left at the base of the hill that leads to a closed yellow gate. Continue on the main dirt road and be alert for a small turnout to the left. It is the parking area I call "Wallman North". It holds 4 trucks and overlooks the railroad tracks. Park there, gear up and walk down the small trail to the tracks that are only 20 yards away. At this point, you can see the river - it's all good!

To get to "Wallman Middle", continue past the first parking area. Proceed down the road for a little over ½ mile and you will see a small dirt road to your left pitching down a steep grade (39.31453,-79.28459). Do not go down that road unless you have a 4x4 vehicle. There is no alternate parking location at this point for a normal flatland car – if you have a flatlander, proceed to Wallman South. One half mile farther south, you enter the formal, large "Wallman South" parking lot. It is marked by a DNR kiosk posted with the regulations and other information for this stretch of the river.

At the southern tip of the lot, there is a rough, pitted road continuing south over the hill. I have not driven down it as it looks exceedingly nasty and there may not be any turnouts allowing you to reverse direction easily. I do not recommend continuing unless you are good at backing up.

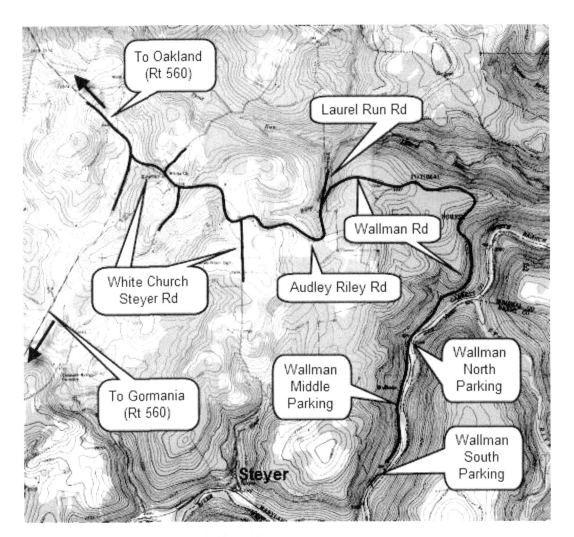

The labels on the map read:

- To Oakland (Rt 560)
- Laurel Run Rd
- Wallman Rd
- White Church Steyer Rd
- Audley Riley Rd
- Wallman North Parking
- Wallman Middle Parking
- Wallman South Parking
- To Gormania (Rt 560)
- Steyer

This sign could not be any smaller. Don't miss it

This is the key turn from White Church-Steyer Road onto Audley Riley Road.

You could easily miss this by continuing around the corner.

Look for the very, very small sign

(39.337617,-79.309831)

North Access Point

Environment and Fish

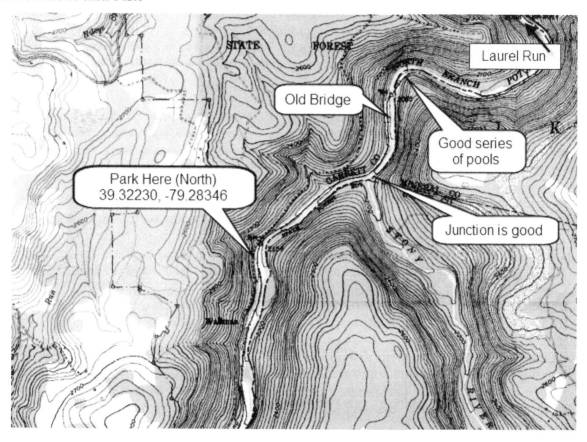

Once you follow the well beaten path from the small parking area to the rail bed, you'll be favorably impressed with the view of the river that unfolds in front of you. Suppress the instant urge to start fishing right there! Wallman is starkly different from the other sections of the river as a result of the canyon cradling the river. The river is much narrower than it is farther downstream with numerous rock ledges and high spots forcing the water into channels terminating in deep pools at each break in the gradient. That same structure makes it tough to find a place to cross the river.

Your best bet for a full day of fishing is to walk a mile and a half downstream to the railroad bridge (39.334414,-79.269576). Fifty yards beyond the bridge is a series of large stepped pools; all are deep.

Those pools are the deepest you'll encounter in this section and are the perfect place to use your sinking tip to get down to the bottom. In addition to trout during the season, there is a good population of smallmouth bass cruising here and looking for trouble.

Wallman

Regulations and property ownership may have changed since publication.
It is your responsibility to know and obey all regulations and not trespass on private property.

87

After you fish the pools, point your rod upstream. Pay good attention to the deep section underneath the railroad bridge. Given the quality of water in these hundred yards, you may spend an hour or two here. At the bridge, the character of the river changes as it tightens and narrows the farther south you move. Look upstream and pick your bank because it will be tough to find places to cross if there is any amount of water crashing down the canyon. The east side features tight vegetation and large boulders pushing to the edge of the river and is definitely "sporty" if the water is high. There is no defined trail. You have to scramble over rocks cruelly placed to inject the most risk into your walk. A quick glance at the topo map confirms that the steep bank forces you to the edge of the river for most of the length.

The west side below the railroad tracks is rough going (do not walk on the tracks). The bottom line is that it is difficult to traverse on either bank and you have to pick your way carefully to dodge huge pockets poison ivy in addition to everything else. If you move up the east side, you should anticipate having to switch banks from time to time as you get closed out by steep rock faces and deep water.

You can spend all day fishing this section -- it's just that good. Around every tight spot that makes it tough to move, there is a deep pool with a gradient break providing the perfect holding position for both trout and smallmouth. Fish these places carefully with nymphs. It's a little more difficult to use spinners in the fast water, but you will find plenty of pools where they can be effective. You can easily work each hole for a half hour or more as you move upstream - so leave yourself plenty of time.

The closer you get to the junction of the North Branch with the Stony River, the deeper the cuts become. In the hundred yards downstream of the junction, there is an additional series of deep, narrow channels as exciting as those near the bridge where you started your day. Be exceptionally cautious because slick, flat rocks defend the water. Their smooth surfaces will cause your cleated wading boots to skid and slip unless you consciously place your foot in cracks as you move around the edge of the water. You may not be aware of these if the water level is high and covering them. You certainly do not want to discover how slick they are by taking a bad slip and ending up in the river.

You will die here without a Wading Staff and must exercise exceptional care with each step; testing each foothold if it looks at all risky before you trust it with your weight.

Above the junction of Stony River, the flow diminishes and it becomes easier to move and fish. However, the banks remain steep and the slick rock shelves become the predominant geological formation. On a normal flow day, they make it easy for you to move up the river, but you have to choose your bank. Be careful to note where the crossing points are as you move because you may have to double back to return to your vehicle.

While the river is narrow here, it is deeply carved as a result of the 24x7 natural "drill" driven by the pressure of the water pushing relentlessly down the canyon. You will find your crossing points limited to the obvious gradient breaks - but even they could be tough to negotiate as a result of the crush of water trying to fit through small spaces.

This is the Wallman North parking area - it's small - you can fit about 4 trucks in here.

The path to the river is off to the left.

This is your first look at the river near the parking area on a misty morning. This is above the junction with Stony River. Note the rock shelf structure that makes it easier to move next to the water.

The river is tight with plenty of runs and good depth. It was running at 86 cfs at the Steyer Gage in this picture. While this may make your fishing adrenalin pump, walk downstream, it gets better.

This is the first pool section downstream of the bridge.

In this picture, the river was running at 207 cfs at the Kitzmiller gage.

The next pool around the bend is this one.

It has a small, deep "lake" extending off to the right – the smallies hug the bottom here.

The last pool in the series of pools before you turn the downstream corner and start heading back to Laurel Run

View looking south from the old bridge support upstream of the bridge.

Note the rocky character of the bank. There is NO easy walking near the river.

The pool depicted was about 2 feet deep on this day and held trout.

Above the junction of Stony River, the North Branch closes in and becomes tight. This looks like the McCloud in California. Close your eyes and you will think you are in the west... but you are only 3 hours away from Washington, DC.

This picture is the McCloud. Amazing similarity!

You must watch water levels! This is a picture of the river when the Kitzmiller gage was running 606 cfs.

While I could make it to the river's edge, the water was running so fast that it was unfishable.

High flows put a significant amount of color in the water that destroys fishing.

Bottom Line

This is a good spot. It's a tough choice between this section and Mile One of Lostland Run. What should tip the scales in your decision calculus are temperature and flow. If you fish anytime past mid-July, come here.

Wallman

Regulations and property ownership may have changed since publication.
It is your responsibility to know and obey all regulations and not trespass on private property.

91

Middle Access Point

Environment and Fish

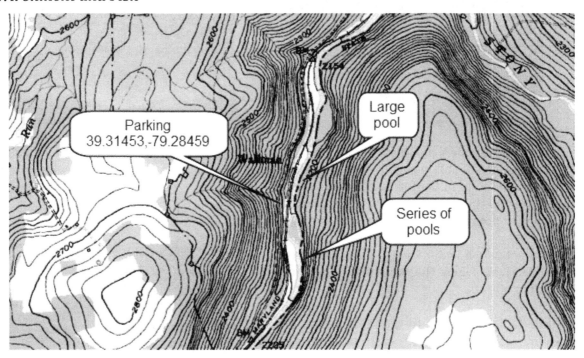

The Wallman Middle access point puts you, obviously, in the middle of the Wallman area. As you look up and downstream you have to decide – "Which direction?" During the summer when the leaves are on the bushes, you'll probably make the wrong decision and begin fishing upstream from the parking lot. Instead, head to the left; walking back towards the Wallman North access point. A quarter-mile downstream, you'll discover the best spot in this section.

There is a deep pool at least 10 to 15 feet deep and approximately 30 feet wide hiding behind a thick line of bushes. It's the biggest you will find in this section of the North Branch. As with all of the river access in this area, you have to exercise considerable care sliding down the steep gravel bank and dodging around the thick bushes mixed with poison ivy to reach the river.

This is fairly easy near the large pool and I recommend you attack it from the downstream side. After you spend some time at the pool, move upstream towards the island separating the river into an east and west branch. The east branch hugs West Virginia and is the better one to fish. It's very tight as a result of the streambed compression forced by the island and the steep hills with the added excitement of a sharp drop in elevation to push the water downstream. There are some small pools behind the major rocks in the stream bed perfect for nymphing.

As you emerge on the southern end of the island, the river widens to 50 to 60 feet across in a broad, medium depth pool. Fish the northern end of the pool before you work your way up the western bank. What you see is typical of the river between this spot and the Wallman South parking area. You can spend a good amount of time in this stretch of the river because of the variety of structure it offers.

The main channel of the river twists and turns around the major ridges of rock and boulders creating a dynamic environment where the fish can be pretty much anywhere. In fact, there are good lips protecting deep spots right before the water plunges over the small line of boulders that divide the pools. Many fishermen ignore the tail of the pools -- here you should take the time and work them carefully. You will find that there are a number of trout, as opposed to smallies, in these deep spots, lying in wait to eat anything floating by. It won't take much of a cast to get these guys. Just drop your fly 10 feet up from the break and let it drift naturally down. With a spinner, throw it far enough upstream to allow the action to start before it hangs on the rock lip.

At the end of the string of pools there's a bend to the right where the river approaches the Wallman South area I discuss in the next section.

View upstream from the entry point at the parking lot (39.31453,-79.28459)

You can see the tip of the island in the middle of the picture

Downstream from the entry point.

This leads down to the large pool shown in the next picture.

The river here is wide and channeled with plenty of good structure to hold fish.

You can work up either bank with no problems.

Wallman
Regulations and property ownership may have changed since publication.
It is your responsibility to know and obey all regulations and not trespass on private property.
93

The large pool that should be your first stop (39.31707,-79.28319)

This is taken from the northern end of the pool looking downstream.

It stretches all the way to the distant rocks at a consistently deep depth.

East branch around the island looking downstream from the southern tip. Wider and greater water volume.

The view upstream from the southern tip of the island.

The river returns to its wider presentation here. The main channel is reasonably deep with plenty of large rocks to break the current.

West branch around the island looking upstream from the northern tip. Narrow. Still a few good spots.

Bottom Line

This is a good spot as a result of the terrain features. The downstream pool continues to be a must visit spot with the best time to visit being a few weeks after stocking. At that point, the normal trout migration following insertion is complete and many of them decide to take up residence here. Beyond the pool, the large island just upstream of the parking area is the dominant terrain feature in the middle section. Since it forces the water into two separate channels, it also reduces the fishable water for about 2/10 of a mile. As a result of this, you can work your way through this section fairly quickly and continue into the Wallman South zone.

South Access Point

Environment and Fish

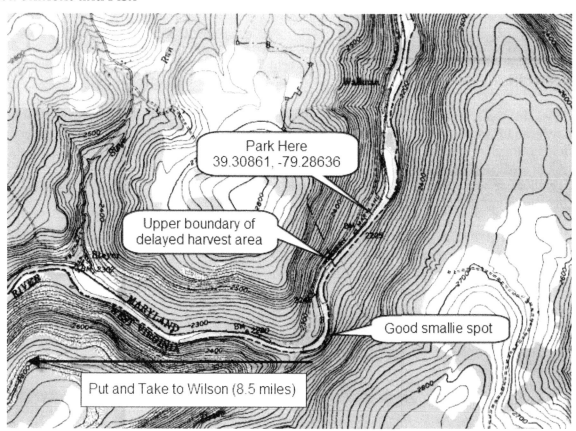

At the Wallman South access point, the North Branch undergoes yet another transition. It reverses from being tight and compressed to gradually widening; becoming calm and flat as it moves up towards Gormania.

When you bounce to a halt in the Wallman South parking lot, there are a couple of things that jump out immediately. The first is the kiosk the Maryland DNR posted that re-emphasizes the regulations in effect for this section of the river. It's a shame they don't have a similar kiosks in each of the other parking lots.

There is an eroded roadbed leading out of the parking lot and up the hill. If you take a close look at your topo map, you may think that following this road will get you to the bend in the river downstream of the Steyer gage. It might. I have not tried to drive my truck on the road as it looks far too narrow for my liking.

The parking lot is a little farther away from the river than in the Wallman North area and you must walk down a well-defined, tight path to get to the river. Be alert for the poison ivy that grows in tight clusters throughout this area and overlaps the trail in many places.

After crossing the rail bed and moving to the river, you discover the flow is not as intense as it is farther downstream. The valley floor has leveled out and, while the river is still fairly narrow, it is wide enough to moderate the intensity of the water.

It's easy to walk along the west bank and you can fish everything from that angle with ease. The west bank features smooth, but slick, rock ledges requiring caution as you walk across them. The east bank is also navigable but closes out in a few places as you move upstream.

Given the level, even flow of the water, it's not surprising this section is marked by longer pools bordered by small gradient breaks. Each of the pools runs fairly deep at 3 to 4 feet in sections and hold both trout (in season) and smallmouth.

As you move upstream, target the obvious places sheltered by fallen trees, overhanging brush and the deeper, more highly oxygenated water that occurs at the head of the pools.

At the bend in the river vicinity 39.30045, -79.28953, there's a 15 foot cliff face on the east bank that shelters a long deep pool. You should flip some terrestrial patterns against the cliff to mimic insects falling from the bank or dredge streamers as deep as you can get them to go. You can sit in that spot and catch five smallies on as many casts on a good day.

There is a longer trail to get to the river from the southern parking lot.

Once you do, you will see a lazy, gentle river.

This picture was taken about ¼ mile upstream from the parking lot. The flow was 86 cfs at the Steyer Gage. Note the smooth rock ledge on the left bank. These extend into the river and minimize the good habitat.

While the flow is the same here as in Wallman North, the water has more places to go and can spread out a bit.

Assuming the stocking season is in the past, there will not be any fish where the bottom is slick and smooth.

The high water in the spring carves out deep cuts next to every rock bank; each demands your attention.

The violent spring flows push trees into the river to form perfect protected habitat for the fish.

You will lose flies and lures on this tree and hear the fish laughing at you as they huddle below in safety.

Looking upstream, the lazy curves in the river indicate a flattening as the river transitions into the level valley leading up to Gormania.

If the water were always crushing, it would blast straight through.

Note that the banks are wide and provide easy walking.

Bottom Line

Easier walking, calmer water and no real evidence of human pressure upstream of the parking lot.

Stony River

Summary Rating

Normal Perspective

Pressure	**Green**	Trout Size	**Red**
Physical Fitness	**Red**	Bass Size	**Yellow**
Access	**Yellow**	Regulations	**Red**
Hard to Find	**Red**	Stocking	**Red**
Scenery	**Green**	**Overall**	**Red**

Aggressive Perspective

Pressure	**Green**	Trout Size	**Red**
Physical Fitness	**Green**	Bass Size	**Yellow**
Access	**Yellow**	Regulations	**Red**
Hard to Find	**Green**	Stocking	**Red**
Scenery	**Green**	**Overall**	**Yellow**

Special Regulations

Since the only way to get to the Stony River is to walk across the North Branch downstream of the Wallman North parking lot, prudence dictates that you follow the regulations in effect for the North Branch. After all, I doubt the Maryland DNR conservation officer will believe you when you say, "I caught this trout on Stony. Honest!" Another point. Since this is in West Virginia, your Maryland license is not valid. The reciprocal agreement only pertains to the North Branch.

The Stony is in the delayed harvest area in the middle of the Wallman section. The delayed harvest area extends upstream to the boundary of the Potomac State Forest near Steyer.

"From June 16 through September 30, the daily creel limit and possession limit is two trout (all species of trout in aggregate). During this period no special bait, lure or tackle restrictions are in effect. From October 1 through June 15, a person may not keep or have any trout in possession while fishing in these areas.

A person may fish only with artificial lures, including artificial flies and streamers. The use or possession of any natural bait, bait fish, fish bait, scents or natural or synthetic devices capable of catching fish other than artificial lures is prohibited."

Regulations and property ownership may have changed since publication.
It is your responsibility to know and obey all regulations and not trespass on private property.

Getting to the Stream

Review the directions for Wallman North. Navigate to Wallman North and park there. But, don't feel too good. You have a ¾ mile hike to get to the entrance of Stony River. Start walking downstream (do not walk on the tracks) until you see Stony River join the North Branch from the east. It's a wide open junction point that is hard to miss. Locate a safe crossing point. Usually, it is easier to cross upstream of the junction. Do not plan on fishing the Stony if you are not capable of making the hike to the junction. You must be strong enough to wade across the river.

Environment and Fish

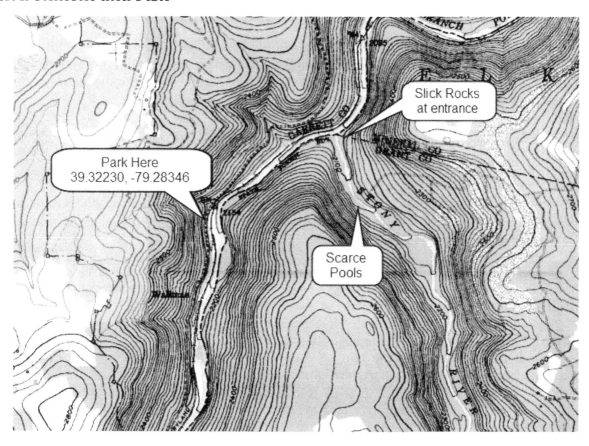

The Stony River is a low gradient stretch of water where you will not see any spectacular plunge pools or white water blasting across rocks. Instead, it's a calm river that winds its way slowly into the North Branch. As such, it adopts the standard pool, run, rifle, pool alternating structure.

Fishing the Stony for trout is problematic. The most compelling issue is Stony River has more than its share of acid runoff and, to date, this has not be mitigated by the addition of lime. Additionally, with over 6 miles of distance for the water to heat up to the point of trout mortality, you may or may not find any stocked trout migrating upstream to escape the heat in the North Branch. I remember measuring the temperature one day in September and discovered that the Stony River was 68 degrees while the North Branch was only 63. That temperature relationship is pretty standard – the

North Branch will run cooler than the Stony except during the core summer months of June, July and August. As you can see from the table below, the season drives the temperature. Bottom line upfront – I am including this coverage to be complete, but you should not drive all the way to the North Branch just to fish the Stony. There is not enough there to make that effort worthwhile.

Mean of monthly values for 5 years of record												
Average F	Jan	Feb	Mar	Apr	May	Jun	Jul	Aug	Sep	Oct	Nov	Dec
Kitzmiller	38.0	35.9	41.9	51.6	58.8	66.7	72.1	72.2	65.6	54.2	45.6	36.7
Stony	39.7	40.3	46.1	54.7	61.5	66.5	70.8	70.0	65.8	54.5	50.4	41.2
Difference	-1.8	-4.4	-4.3	-3.1	-2.7	0.2	1.3	2.3	-0.2	-0.3	-4.8	-4.5

The first thing you notice as you walk into the Stony is the opening is protected by broad ledges of flat, slick rocks. You need to be exceptionally careful as you navigate across the shelves; move cautiously with a low center of gravity or you will find yourself with feet in the air, bouncing off the rocks and nurturing a sore tailbone for the rest of the day.

Immediately upstream of the junction, you encounter the first broad pool. It is sheltered on both sides by tall trees and runs about 3 feet deep. I have seen trout holding in that pool in the middle of summer.

Continuing, the river separates into two channels with the deeper channel on the left. It maintains that fractured character for quite a while with the water running randomly, forcing you to look for cuts around rocks deep enough to hold fish.

The river remains nondescript until you get about ¾ mile upstream. There is a medium sized pool backed up behind a small waterfall. This is as far as I have gone given the better fishing available on the main stem of the North Branch.

There is no other good access to the river other than from the North Branch. The next point upstream is where Route 50 runs across the Stony as you leave Gormania heading to Romney. There is a large parking area there, but it is plastered with "posted" signs.

Picture taken looking south (upstream) on the North Branch.

The junction to the Stony is on the left at the top of the rocks.

You can see the rock shelves at the entrance. Use them as a landmark.

Here is the Stony, looking upstream from the junction.

The rock shelves continue and create some nice small pools.

The flow measured at the Mt Storm gage on the Stony was 34 cfs when I took this picture.

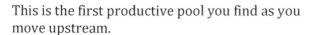

View looking downstream to the North Branch at the entrance of the Stony (the Stony is behind the camera).

Be especially careful of these slick rocks. They are dangerous even when dry.

The pool shown to the left is a good, deep run.

This is the first productive pool you find as you move upstream.

It is sheltered by trees and remains cool.

I have seen trout in this spot in the middle of summer.

Bottom line

With the North Branch being as attractive as it is, the Stony is not a destination I recommend. You should only fish this river if you are curious and have had your fill on the North Branch.

Gormania

Summary Rating

Normal Perspective

Pressure	**Red**	Trout Size	**Green**
Physical Fitness	**Green**	Bass Size	**Yellow**
Access	**Yellow**	Regulations	**Red**
Hard to Find	**Green**	Stocking	**Green**
Scenery	**Yellow**	**Overall**	**Yellow**

Aggressive Perspective

Pressure	**Red**	Trout Size	**Green**
Physical Fitness	**Red**	Bass Size	**Yellow**
Access	**Yellow**	Regulations	**Red**
Hard to Find	**Red**	Stocking	**Green**
Scenery	**Yellow**	**Overall**	**Red**

Special Regulations

None – this is a "Put and Take" area from the uppermost boundary of Potomac State Forest at Wallman upstream approximately 8.5 miles to the bridge at Old Wilson Road.

On most maps, Gormania is called "Gormania", but you may also see this small town referred to as "Gorman". The difference? Gormania is on the West Virginia side of the bridge and Gorman is on the Maryland side. Since Gormania is the most common map name, that's what I use.

All the fishing in this section requires crossing private property. According to the DNR, that is OK unless you see a posted sign. Frankly, this part of the North Branch is horrible... do not bother with it. If many of the landowners post their property, the DNR will no longer stock this stretch. Be alert for that. Again, go somewhere else on the river.

Getting to the Stream

From Gormania, head north on Route 560. Take an immediate right onto Steyer-Gorman Road after you cross the bridge. Follow this road until it cuts north where it joins White Church Steyer Road (39.304683,-79.311912). This is the eastern end of this section and you can access the river from here.

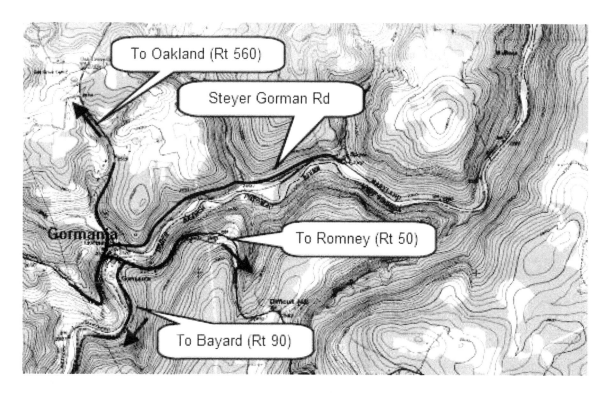

In addition to going all the way to the end of the road, you can pull off and fish the North Branch at any number of places between Route 560 in Gormania and the end of the Steyer-Gorman Road. There are plenty of turnouts and many offer easy access to the river as long as the access has not been posted.

For sure, there is one section of posted private property between Gormania and Steyer on the river side of the road. The driveway looks like a turnoff to the river. Be alert for the "posted" and "private drive" signs when you get into the vicinity of 39.302229,-79.325092.

Access Point:
- Railroad tracks near White Church Steyer Road (39.30475,-79.31246)
- Numerous turnouts along Steyer-Gorman Road

Environment and Fish

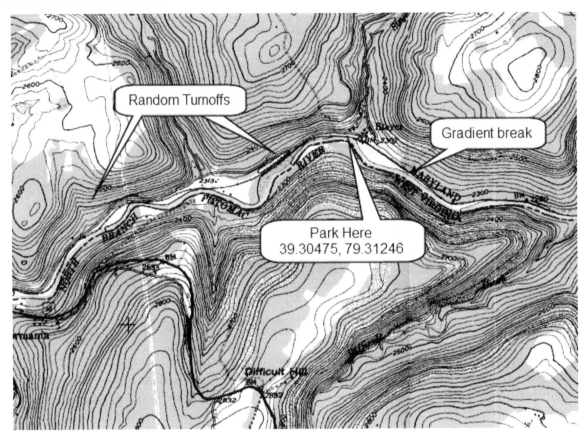

After parking at the end of the Steyer-Gorman Road, you can either walk downstream towards the Potomac State Forest and the delayed harvest area or upstream towards Gormania. There is a faint fisherman's trail next to the river, but it will eventually run out and you have to either wade in the river or bushwhack through some high brush.

The river is broad and reasonably deep when the flow is up. In the spring, in the midst of the normal stocking season, expect to have plenty of water with the typical depth being 2 to 3 feet. As the water levels abate with the summer heat, the going gets easier. Given the width of the river, there are no significant landmarks to guide you to any particular spot. When you fish here, you have to feel your way downstream and identify the hotspots based on the character of the river on the day you are there.

As you move upstream beyond Steyer, the river remains broad with a rocky bottom. The deeper channels are randomly distributed and the location is dependent on the water volume. The only way to discover these is to fish the river and look for the darker shade of water indicating a deeper spot. The bends in the river are obvious deep spots and you should fish them if they have not been posted. The first good bend is at 39.30216,-79.31956 as you move upstream.

There are plenty of overhanging trees and bushes to provide welcome shade for the fish and great targets for terrestrial patterns. The river maintains this look until it reaches 39.30099,-79.32723 where the bottom structure moves from rock to sand. The sand stretch is a dead zone. Skip it and rejoin the river where it moves back to rock at 39.30030,-79.33181. If not posted, fish the bend and upstream until the sand reappears at 39.29771.-79.33722. The bottom remains sandy until you reach the outskirts of Gormania. Like other sections of the North Branch, your success will depend on flow. If there has been a recent storm, you can count on water levels returning to normal in about 4 days with the total volume of flow dropping by half from the storm surge peak in 2 days. This is important to factor into your fishing trip if you see rain in the forecast a few days before you arrive.

Check the Steyer gage after the rain and take note of the reading. Based on a few sample sets of readings I looked at, the flow is approximately 55% of the peak the following day, 45% on the second day and 30% on the third day; tailing off to normal after that.

Looking east from 39.302092,-79.308372 downstream towards the Potomac State Forest. This is close to bottom of the Gormania section. The bend in the distance is the upper end of the coverage of Wallman South.

The river begins to change as it enters the Wallman section. Downstream there are more gradient breaks with riffles and spot pools. The river is wide, broad, and has a nice current. Typically, it is 3 feet deep or better when the Steyer gage runs at 200 cfs.

View looking upstream from 39.30352,-79.312255

This is at the end of the Steyer-Gorman road looking back towards Gormania.

On this day, Steyer gage was 203 cfs right after a storm.

Note all the slit in the river – any storm will kick up slit and darken the water.

Gormania

Regulations and property ownership may have changed since publication.
It is your responsibility to know and obey all regulations and not trespass on private property.

105

Picture taken from 39.304782,-79.314337 looking back to Steyer.

The river bottom is rocky, but not as tough to wade as it is in the Potomac State Forest.

Flow measured at the Steyer gage was 76 cfs.

Looking upstream from 39.300249, -79.332211 (about halfway between Route 50 and the end of the road).

There are no gradient changes to produce whitewater in this section.

The bottom here is mostly sand.

The Steyer gage was running at 64 cfs on the day this picture was taken.

Closer to Gormania, the river transitions back to a rocky bottom.

Skip the sandy middle; it will be a dead zone.

Bottom Line

This section is a backup fishing spot if you want an easier wading experience. There are not as many boulders and rocks in the river as you will find downstream. You still need a wading staff because your feet will always find that one place where you will slip and pitch forward into the water without the benefit of additional support. This area is very close to the population centers and experiences plenty of pressure. However, once the trout season winds down, you will probably have this section of the river to yourself – but... it will not be worth it   as a result of the private property issues and the small number of trout stocked here.

Bayard

Summary Rating

Normal Perspective

Pressure	**Red**	Trout Size	**Green**
Physical Fitness	**Green**	Bass Size	**Red**
Access	**Green**	Regulations	**Red**
Hard to Find	**Green**	Stocking	**Green**
Scenery	**Red**	**Overall**	**Red**

Aggressive Perspective

Pressure	**Red**	Trout Size	**Green**
Physical Fitness	**Red**	Bass Size	**Red**
Access	**Red**	Regulations	**Red**
Hard to Find	**Red**	Stocking	**Green**
Scenery	**Red**	**Overall**	**Red**

Special Regulations

None – this is a "Put and Take" from the uppermost boundary of Potomac State Forest at Wallman upstream approximately 8.5 miles to the bridge at Old Wilson Road.

Getting to the Stream

The first question you should ask yourself is, "Why bother?" This section is the matching lousy bookend that pairs with Westernport/Piedmont 30 miles downstream.

Yes, the river is stocked from the Wilson Bridge down to Gormania. In fact, the section is stocked at the Wilson Bridge, Bayard and two additional places between Bayard and Gormania.

But this is just nasty water. The entire section from Steyer up to the Wilson Bridge only receives 7% of the total trout stocked in the North Branch. While I do not know the specific calculus the Maryland DNR follows to decide where to plant the fish, it appears to me the environment is better for the trout from Gormania to Steyer and that is where I would expect the heaviest stocking. When you look at the water upstream of Gormania, you will understand why I reach that conclusion.

Assuming you want to fish it, stay on Route 50 west from Gormania, WV and go up the hill. At the bend in the hill, turn left onto Althouse Hill Road and follow it down into the valley. Althouse Hill Road parallels the river up to the inoperable bridge at Bayard.

Access Point:
- Turnout on Althouse Road (39.285326,-79.351494, 39.278139,-79.356417)
- Bridge at Bayard (39.273727,-79.369676)
- Bridge at Wilson 39.253624,-79.398601

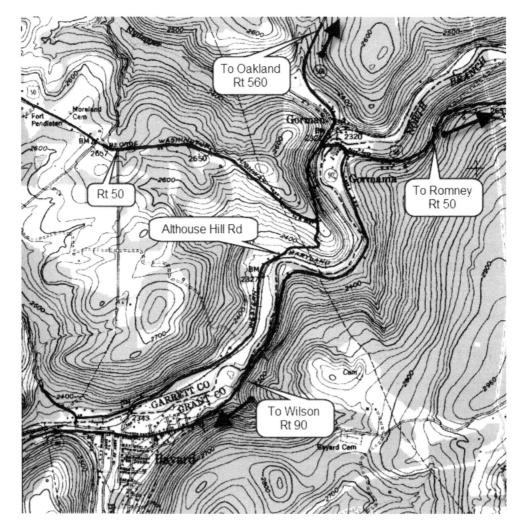

You can see the river from Althouse Hill Road and should be able to find turnoffs where you can access the river. Again, private property prevails so be alert for any posted signs.

Note that this stretch of the North Branch is in a populated area. If they even exist, the leash laws are not enforced and you may encounter dogs who will not be happy to see you. In particular, be aware of this near and around the bridge at Bayard. Take your pepper spray with you.

Environment and Fish

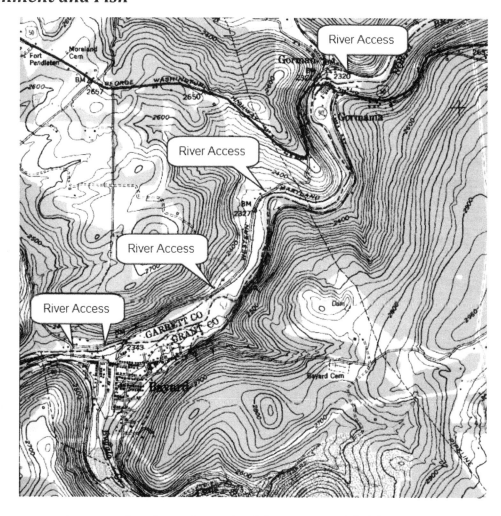

The river resumes its normal rocky trait south of Gormania and holds that look all the way up to Wilson with the exception of a few sandy sections. Most of the water is near Gormania; the river narrows and becomes shallow upstream from the town.

As you move upstream towards Wilson, the river remains uniform in depth and width until you get to the bridge at Bayard. It widens here slightly, limiting the fishing to those places where water can collect in holes and cuts.

The only dependable access to the river is from the Maryland side. The West Virginia bank is protected by innumerable "posted" signs. While you can find a few breaks to park and walk to the river, you may as well fish this from the Maryland side. In Maryland, the places to get to the river are obvious and near the road. Park in an available turnoff and walk to the river. While you will not see "stocked trout water" signs, the Maryland Freshwater Fisheries team responsible for the Western Region (301-334-8218) assured me that the area is stocked and accessible to the public. As long as you do not see a "posted" sign, you can fish.

When you approach the river, the first thing that jumps out is the striking red color of the river bottom stained by years of mining operations leaching acid into the river. As discussed earlier, the acid is under control and there is a doser upstream of Wilson that constantly adds buffering chemicals to keep the pH in a range that promotes fish survival. The banks are easy to negotiate. You will not have to scramble to get into the river. The rocky river bottom will continue to make wading an exercise in caution – stay alert!

Looking upstream towards Bayard at 39.27807,-79.35644

Note the flat perspective. The river does not have a significant amount of velocity as it spreads in the valley below Gormania.

The banks are not steep and you can move in and out easily.

View upstream from 39.27445,-79.36681

In the summer, the vegetation shelters the banks, but it's not worth fishing up here as most of the water is gone by then.

Upstream from the bridge at Bayard at 39.273727,-79.369676

I took this picture in March. By late April, you will see more rocks than water.

Note the bright red, acid-stained rocks.

Downstream from the bridge at Wilson at 39.253624,-79.398601

This is one of the places where the Maryland DNR stocks. The fish go into this pool and, after a few days, may migrate downstream up to 500 yards depending on the amount of water available to support their exodus.

Bottom Line

I have to admit that I have never been motivated to fish this part of the river. When presented with the opportunity to fish here or anywhere else in Garrett County, I always go elsewhere. While the water here can support trout as a result of the lime doser upstream of Wilson, it is just not a pleasant place to fish. In addition, the water is undependable and can turn to a trickle by May.

You may want to drive by and flip a fly just to complete your total North Branch experience, but it's just not worth it to me.

Garrett County Trout Streams

Bear Creek

Approximate Boundary: 39.654408,-79.330069 to 39.660718,-79.396361 (4.45 miles)

Type: Put and Take

Directions:
East: From I-68, take exit 14A to merge onto US 219S. Turn right on Bear Creek Road. The stocked section starts approximately 1.6 miles from the junction of Bear Creek Road and US 219.

West: From I-68, take exit 4 to merge onto Friendsville Road. Turn left onto 1st Avenue. Turn right on Maple Street. Maple turns into Bear Creek Road. The stocked section begins on the east side of I-68 where the road crosses the creek.

Access Point: Various turnoffs on Bear Creek Road to include: 39.6554,-79.30426, 39.66028,-79.3163, 39.65695,-79.35625, 39.65767,-79.3586, 39.65835,-79.36073, 39.65653,-79.36457, 39.65859,-79.36878, 39.65585,-79.38821, 39.65377,-79.38399, 39.65308,-79.38511, 39.65396,-79.38659, 39.65542,-79.3885, 39.65593,-79.39149, 39.66095,-79.39686

At the time of publication, there is a disconnect between the published boundary of the stocked section and the reality on the ground. I extracted the boundary GPS coordinates from what was published by the DNR on the Internet. However, on the ground, the first DNR signage actually occurs a little over a quarter mile west of US 219, not 1.6 miles from the landmark as quoted above. Therefore, the fishable stretch of Bear Creek extends beyond 4.45 miles - all scenic, all good. Do not bother to fish east of US 219, it is all posted. At the narrow headwaters near the first turnoff, there is room for two cars to park. It runs 25 feet wide over a bottom composed of small rocks with a minimum of sand.

Gradient breaks occur at regular intervals, producing deep spots below the riffles as the creek drops almost 800 feet between US 219 and the I-68 bridge. After that first opportunity to fish, the road moves away from the creek, gaining altitude and limiting admittance. To fish the western stretch, anglers must walk from the small turnoff with no easy path along the creek. The next access point is east of the junction of Harmons Road (39.66028,-79.3163) and features another two car turnout. It is set back from the river with a well-defined path to the creek. The amount of flow increases as a result of the contributions of two small streams feeding in from the north. Bear Creek now runs 30 feet wide with an increasing number of rocks and boulders strewn across the streambed. Shoreline vegetation lightens, making movement along the northern bank much easier – especially 20 yards back from the creek where the forest thins out. The southern bank runs along the precipitous mountainside that leads up to Hickory Ridge and Wagner Hill.

The road resumes its upward climb and the creek is not approachable until the road drops around the corner near a sparsely populated residential section in the vicinity of Everly Road. Given the obvious issues with private property, continue to follow the road until it enters the narrow gap between Winding Ridge and Oak Hill. For the next mile, there are scattered, small turnoffs with the largest one able to accommodate six vehicles. It is immediately prior to the sharp left where the protruding ridgeline pokes to the south off Winding Ridge.

There is plenty of good fishing in this stretch with one spot being the deep pool next to a supersized boulder close to the large parking area. A small ATV trail runs next to the river for a short distance and connects anglers to good holes in both directions. The southern bank remains relatively inaccessible as it continues to be braced by the mountainside. Movement is easy through the flat forest along the northern shore.

Once "civilization" returns, parking opportunities disappear until the road takes a sharp turn to the right near Friendsville with the junction of Bear Creek Road and Accident Friendsville Road being a significant landmark. The creek flows deep and wide with plenty of room for vehicles in well-spaced turnoffs along both roads (Accident Friendsville Road is on the south side of the creek). In fact, one of the most popular places to fish is immediately downstream of the junction where there is a series of stairstep pools that extend west approximately 100 yards. Immediately after stocking, this is where you will see plenty of anglers.

Bridge at Friendsville-Addison Road

Below the bridge

As the creek moves through another drop in elevation, it tightens again, offering deep water with rhododendrons packing both sides. The next parking is at the bridge crossing over Bear Creek where there is room for two cars to pull off on the side of the road. Upstream, the river runs down a drop in elevation to create an additional staircase of pocket water marked by medium-size boulders. Downstream, the number of pools increases as the stream moves underneath the I-68 bridge (a few parking spots) and begins to parallel Walnut Street. At that point, there is urban roadside parking next to a gentle, grassy slope.

Bear Creek is the third most heavily stocked stream in the State.

Big Run

Approximate Boundary: 39.543268,-79.138516 to 39.603043,-79.167831 (5.11 miles)

Type: Zero Creel

Directions: From Westernport, take MD 135 west towards Bloomington. Turn right onto Savage River Road. Turn left on Big Run Road.

Access Point: Various turnoffs and campsites adjacent to Big Run Road

Big Run drops 1,162 feet as it wanders 5.1 miles from its source on the south side of Meadow Mountain through the gap between Middle and Peapatch Ridges. Given that huge drop, Big Run meets all expectations for a high gradient stream and pairs up with its major tributary, Monroe Run, to be the key water feature inside Big Run State Park. The DNR stocked almost 17,000 brook trout in the 40 years between 1948 and 1988 to reestablish their presence. Like the rest of the Savage Reservoir watershed, it is protected by a Zero Creel fishing regulation. The name "Big Run" is an appellation that recognizes the width of the stream rather than the depth. In most places, the shallow stream runs 15 to 20 feet wide across a rocky bed. Given the sharp drop in elevation, anglers must hike to find pools deep enough to hold fish. Most of the park facilities are located at the junction of Big Run Road and Savage River Road and include improved campsites, restrooms and a potable water source.

Near the Savage Reservoir

Farther upstream

Crabtree Creek

Approximate Boundary: 39.503974,-79.155296 to 39.457684,-79.226967 (4.85 miles)

Type: Zero Creel

Directions

From Westernport, take MD 135 west towards Bloomington. Turn right onto Savage River Road. At the first hard, hairpin turn at the west end of the reservoir, take a right onto Spring Lick Road. Crabtree Creek runs on the south side of the road.

Access Point: Various turnouts along Spring Lick Road to include 39.49994,-79.16156, 39.49924,-79.16175, 39.49439,-79.16781, 39.49187,-79.17212

Crabtree Creek rivals Middle Fork as a top brook trout fishing destination. It runs wide and clear across a rocky bottom that provides ideal habitat for brook trout. In fact, this is one of the streams identified in the Maryland DNR Brook Trout Management Plan as having a robust, self-sustaining brook trout population. Please obey the Zero Creel limit admonishments that the DNR posts at all of the turnouts! As you drive up Spring Lick Road, the

Regulations and property ownership may have changed since publication.
It is your responsibility to know and obey all regulations and not trespass on private property.

creek scratches its course through dramatic scenery that includes deep runs and plunge pools. Avoid fishing near any of the residential areas even if they are not specifically posted.

Near reservoir

Plenty of good pools

The Potomac State Forest lies to the south of the creek and includes the land between the mountain and the road for the first 1,400 feet of the stream. At approximately 39.501011,-79.159781, the creek flows through private property with angler access permitted at landowner discretion. As of early 2011, there are no "posted" signs adjacent to the DNR turnoffs identified above. In addition, DNR signage is at each location, confirming access, *for now*. I urgently request anglers to be gentle with this stream, leave no trace, pick up any garbage you see and do everything you can to protect it.

Risky road leading to stream

Next to road

The Potomac State Forest northern boundary runs along the old rail bed that rides a precarious ridgeline on the northern side of Backbone Mountain. There is a gap in public ownership starting at 39.480759,-79.185426 extending to 39.468402,-79.201047. However, according to American Whitewater, aggressive kayakers plop their boats into the creek at the bridge using the railroad right-of-way at the town of Swanton. In the past, they reported friction with one of the landowners in that area. But, since railroad property is automatically posted, avoid this access.

Exercise caution on how you enter the water since the Potomac State Forest property does not begin until 39.457071,-79.221261, approximately 0.3 miles east from the bridge. Any creek that gets kayakers excited based on the number of ledges and drops is usually a good indicator of promising water for hiking anglers once the level drops enough to make the stream uninteresting to kayak borne adrenaline junkies.

For those who enter the creek from the Savage River Reservoir side, the best turnoff is 1,000 feet prior to Spring Lick Road taking an abrupt bend to the north. Do not be tempted to follow the old road adjacent to the bend that hangs off the ledge leading to the creek. It is narrow, severely eroded and while you might be able to drive to edge of the creek, chances are you may find yourself upside down instead of right side up when the fragile roadbed collapses under the weight of your vehicle. At this spot, Spring Lick Run slams into Crabtree Creek and creates a set of good pools that will, appropriately, lure you farther west into the deep gorge between the surrounding mountains.

In the gorge

Robust flow, high gradient

Dry Run

Approximate Boundary: 39.523078,-79.144485 to 39.537278,-79.158347 (1.76 miles)

Type: Zero Creel

Directions: From Westernport, take MD 135 west towards Bloomington. Turn right onto Savage River Road. Turn left onto Dry Run Road.

Access Point: Single turnoff on Dry Run Road (39.52355,-79.14719)

Garrett County Trout Streams

Regulations and property ownership may have changed since publication.
It is your responsibility to know and obey all regulations and not trespass on private property.

117

Dry Run drops 670 feet into the gash between Solomon Ridge and Mount Nebo. The stark terrain creates an abrupt canyon that squeezes the creek and the road beside it into a tight, thin line with limited parking. Other than at the confluence with the Savage River Reservoir, the only convenient turnoff is at 39.52355,-79.14719, merely 500 feet from the intersection with Savage River Road.

In fact, once past 39.52488,-79.15022, the road rises sharply to claw its way along the southern hillside, moving far away from the valley floor and the trickling creek below. While the creek remains fishable upstream from that point, it is up to you to decide how much sweat to invest to find the widely distributed pools. In the lower reaches, the creek ranges up to ten feet wide, compressing to a small dribble no more than two feet across in the higher elevations. The water runs across a freestone bottom flecked with large rocks surrounded by cobble.

Elk Lick

Approximate Boundary: 39.60175,-79.08742 to 39.620202,-79.113114 (2.41 miles)

Type: Zero Creel

Directions: From Westernport, take MD 135 west towards Bloomington. Turn right onto Savage River Road.

Access Point: Elk Lick Campsite (39.60175,-79.08742)

Tumbling 556 feet across its 2.4 mile course inside the Savage River State Forest, the creek does not pause to create many fishable pools. Look for the start of the State property on Elk Lick Road and pull off at the campsite located just northwest of the park border. From there, walk over to the stream and slide down the ten foot tall bank to reach the water's edge. It is not wide and the terrain only allocates five to ten feet to hold the streambed. The hillside is steep; prepare to sweat to find a fishable pool.

Herrington Creek

Approximate Boundary: 39.460517,-79.447271 to 39.461031,-79.423302 (1.73 miles)

Type: Put and Take

Directions:
North: From I-68, take exit 4 onto MD 42. Follow MD 42W to the intersection with Blooming Rose Road and turn left to go back underneath the Interstate. Turn left on White Rock Road. Turn right onto Cranesville Road. Cranesville Road becomes Herrington Manor Road. Park either at the dam inside the State Park or go past the entrance to the State Park to the large parking area on the north side of the creek.

South: From Oakland, turn west on E Center Street. Follow it through the intersection with N Bradley Lane onto Bradley Lane to turn right on Liberty Street. Head west on Liberty Street across the river and into the park. The name of the road changes to Herrington Manor Road. The large parking area is on the north side of the creek prior to reaching the entrance to the State Park. Another option is to park near the dam in the State Park.

Access Point:
- Parking lot on the east side of Herrington Manor Road adjacent to the creek (39.464106,-79.443864)
- Herrington Manor Lake Road near the north end of Herrington Lake (39.459146,-79.449607)

Herrington Creek is lightly stocked for its length, only receiving 480 fish in the Spring season, but all those fish are inserted in a very small area. A DNR kiosk marks the large turnout on the north side of the creek. There are no trails paralleling the stream downstream other than the faint fisherman's trail that leads directly from the parking area to the water. At the turnout, the creek is approximately 15 feet wide and thoroughly overgrown with dense vegetation. The stream bottom is a mix of sand, rocks and small boulders.

The upstream side is tied into the formal trail network of the Herrington Manor State Park and offers easier access where the trail parallels the creek. Between the dam on Herrington Lake and the turnout, the stream is low gradient, flowing through an open valley. After crossing the road, the elevation drops approximately 40 feet in the 1.4 mile stretch to the junction of the Youghiogheny River. Unlike the upstream section, downstream runs through a deep valley with no exit point other than the original turnout. The most dramatic section begins 0.8 miles from the road.

According to the Eastern Brook Trout Venture, Herrington Creek has good enough water quality, equivalent to the Savage Reservoir watershed, to support natural reproduction of trout. However, the DNR 2005 Brook Trout Management Plan did not identify this creek as having a self-sustaining population. Maybe that will change in the future, but it means that if you hike a significant distance from the road, you may not encounter any fish.

Middle Fork

Approximate Boundary: 39.512683,-79.154227 to 39.51447,-79.216068 (5.32 miles)

Type: Zero Creel

Directions: From Westernport, take MD 135 west towards Bloomington. Turn right onto Savage River Road. Middle Fork crosses Savage River Road north of the junction of Spring Lick Road.

Access Point:
- Small roadside turnout at the Middle Fork bridge (39.512683,-79.154227)
- Dry Run Road (not personally confirmed - 39.54982,-79.17637)

Dropping 871 feet, Middle Fork starts in the Middle Fork Wildland and ends at the Savage River Reservoir. The stream is famous enough to be written up in Ann McIntosh's book, *Mid-Atlantic Budget Angler*. According to her, there are 2,400 trout per mile, making this top producing water. A key reason for that vibrant population may be the long hike to reach the best water cradled in the deep valley of the Middle Fork Wildland. There is no easy choice since you must choose between a grueling 45 minute hike from the top via a gate on the south side of Dry Run Road near 39.54982,-79.17637 (not personally confirmed) or a two-mile walk from the parking area near the reservoir.

Lower section

Below the road intersection

As with all of the Zero Creel water feeding the reservoir, Middle Fork runs through a tight cut between two large mountains - Mount Nebo to the north and Chestnut Knob to the south. It is a mountain freestone stream that varies in width depending whether you are near the headwaters or at the junction with the reservoir. At its confluence with the Savage River Reservoir, the creek can run 30 feet across during periods of high water. At the end of a dry summer, the flow reduces to a mere trickle or even disappears, with trout desperately trying to survive, huddled in widely spaced community pools. Other than the large rocks and steep cliffs that demand careful movement, the creek side vegetation is not oppressive and will not be a major obstacle to a stealthy approach or an accurate cast. The initial path from the Savage River access point is wide for the first half mile before it degenerates into a typical hiking trail. This is remote country. Be prepared for anything as you move farther and farther away from the road.

Regulations and property ownership may have changed since publication.
It is your responsibility to know and obey all regulations and not trespass on private property.

| Above the road intersection | Same location as the cover picture in a dry year |

Muddy Creek

Approximate Boundary: 39.500878,-79.416329 to 39.519801,-79.477934 (5.13 miles)

Type: Put and Take

Directions:
North: From Deep Creek Lake, head southwest on US 219S/Garrett Highway. Turn right onto Mayhew Inn Road. Turn left onto Oakland Sang Run Road. Turn right onto Swallow Falls Road. After crossing the bridge over the river, turn right onto Maple Glade Road.

South: From Oakland, take MD 39W. Turn right onto Oakland Rosedale Road. Follow it through several turns. Turn left onto Liberty Street. The name of the street changes to Herrington Manor Road. Turn right onto Swallow Falls Road. Turn left to enter the park on Maple Glade road.

Access Point: Swallow Falls State Park (39.499206,-79.419057)

The Maryland DNR teamed up with the Youghiogheny Trout Unlimited Chapter and Garrett College to dump limestone into the stream to mitigate acid deposition to support a year-round fishery. Begun in 1999, the recovery program continues with tons of limestone placed in the stream over the years. The successful program allows the DNR to stock "put and grow" brown trout fingerlings. Therefore, in addition to the stocked fish that may have drawn you to this spot in the first place, you may end up tangling with cranky wild browns.

Others have noted, and I will add my voice to theirs, that Muddy Creek must have been named by an angler intent on protecting spectacular fishing water by giving it the most boring name imaginable. After all, it conjures up visions of a slow-moving, silt filled backwater that would be the last place in the world to fish for trout. Perhaps the name was assigned by an early settler gazing at the languid drip of the stream running across a muddy bottom as it exited the Pine Swamp complex on the West Virginia border. From there, the creek runs through a wide valley hemmed in by Snaggy Mountain to the south and Lewis Knob to the north. While this stretch is theoretically within the extent of the stocked section, there is no place to turn off the road and no DNR signage indicating that it is stocked water.

Unless you want to see the muddy trickle at the top end, do not bother to drive farther north than the Swallow Falls State Park since all the roads that could lead over to the creek are gated or posted. Considering this, you are bound to wonder about how the DNR stocks the creek given the distance from traditional stocking points at bridge crossings. According to the Park Ranger I discussed this with, they use ATVs and manpower to spread the fish.

The creek undergoes a dramatic transformation from muddy top to rocky bottom as it plunges over 200 feet in elevation from Cranesville Road to the Muddy Creek Falls. After paying the fee to enter the park, pull into the lot and walk through the arch at the northeast corner to transition onto the well-developed, easy walking trail system that not only leads to the upper and lower Swallow Falls on the Youghiogheny River, but also to the Muddy Creek Falls and the great fishing upstream.

Within a few steps of leaving the parking lot, the roar of multiple waterfalls assaults your ears. Since the Muddy Creek Falls is the highest freefalling waterfall in the State, it is well worth the 10 minute diversion to throw a glance and take a picture. Continue down the wooded path to the observation platform overlooking the falls for the best view. Once you make your mother proud by completing that obligatory cultural diversion, follow the rough, three foot wide path to the next bridge upstream.

Your casting arm will begin to twitch as your eyes touch the 30 to 40 foot wide free-flowing stream roiling crystal-clear over a rocky bottom. Spectacular water! Cross the bridge and use the rough fisherman's trail along the west bank.

Unfortunately, the trail is only good to move from point to point since dense vegetation lines both banks, forcing you onto the narrow, rock lined shoreline or into the creek itself to actually fish.

Exercise considerable caution when the creek is running high since American Whitewater advertises that Muddy Creek can offer a class V whitewater experience in the lower reaches.

Poplar Lick Run

Approximate Boundary: 39.58434,-79.09181 to 39.631903,-79.12277 (6.4 miles)

Type: Zero Creel

Directions: From Westernport, take MD 135 west towards Bloomington. Turn right onto Savage River Road. Look for the kiosk that marks the trailhead approximately five miles north of Big Run Road.

Access Point:
- Marked trailhead on Savage River Road (39.58434,-79.09181)
- Parking lot at the south end of the lake in New Germany State Park (39.632862,-79.122316)

Poplar Lick is best known for the off-road vehicle trail that parallels its path. The ORV trail is permanently closed and, to the delight of trout hikers, the only way to fish this long stream is to hike or bike in. Since the trail is actually the remnants of an old Civilian Conservation Corps roadway built during the depression in 1934, walking is easy along the hard-packed surface. The trail winds its way back and forth across the stream 13 times with only five bridges, allowing you to go as far upstream as you care to, adding distance between where you stand and your personal perception of where the fishing pressure begins.

There are numerous primitive campsites adjacent to the trail, just be sure to self-register before you begin your trek.

Although Point Ridge looms dramatically above the streambed with the contour lines on the topographic map being close enough to make you cross eyed, Poplar Lick only drops 800 feet from its start at the base of New Germany Lake. This makes for easy hiking and biking. Like its brook trout friendly neighbors to the south, Poplar Lick is a mountain freestone stream with a good surge of water allowing it to expand to 30 feet wide at the base. There are a passel of pools that hold trout. In addition to brook trout, there are stocked trout, browns and rainbows that run up from the Savage River in search of cool water.

Casselman River

Approximate Boundary: 39.694782,-79.139265 to 39.722427,-79.111716 (4.1 miles)
DNR Guidance: From a red post located on the south side of the I-68 eastbound bridge downstream to the Pennsylvania State Line.

Type: Delayed Harvest

Directions:
From I-68, take exit 19 onto MD 495N/Bittinger Road towards Grantsville. Turn right on US 40 Alt E/Main Street. Turn left into the Casselman Bridge State Park parking area prior to crossing the river or proceed across the river and turn right into the parking adjacent to I-68. To fish downstream, continue east on Main Street and turn left on River Road. River Road parallels the river.

Access Point:
- Casselman Bridge State Park parking (39.696274,-79.144777)
- I-68 lot parking (39.695299,-79.140611)
- River Road bridge parking (39.702179,-79.136712)
- Various turnoffs along River Road (last one at 39.716144,-79.120648)

Fishing on the Casselman River was destroyed in the 1800s by acid runoff from mining. The DNR corrected this through aggressive management and reclamation efforts and, by 1989, the river had become a "go to" trout fishing destination. The great joy of the Casselman as opposed to its siblings farther to the west, the North Branch of the Potomac and the Savage River, is that wading is much easier. The "rock snot" that forms a treacherous coating over every rock in the other two rivers is not as prevalent on the Casselman. The smaller rocks and cobble that form the streambed are a refreshing change from the larger boulders on the other rivers that were designed by the devil to twist ankles and pitch anglers head first into icy water.

While the Casselman has plenty of large rocks, they serve the positive purpose of creating holding areas for fish rather than obstacles for anglers. Although the river is narrow as it winds its way underneath the I-68 bridge, it quickly grows from 20 to over 80 feet as it enters the flat farmland upstream of the Pennsylvania State line. Sadly, the river warms to the point of trout mortality in the summer, so reserve time on your cold weather calendar to fish when the DNR stocks the river with large numbers of brown and rainbow trout, including many of trophy size. As the weather and the water warms up, the trout migrate to the cool water trickling into the river from a few random springs. If you can find those, you can find late-season fish.

The local Trout Unlimited chapter is active in supporting the DNR by float stocking the river. Therefore, it pays to walk away from the road. Start your day in the four acre Casselman River Bridge State Park. The manicured grounds make fishing easy. Once south of the US 40 bridge, the bank becomes a steep, jumbled cluster of large rocks making it tough to negotiate unless you wade. To fish that side, start from the I-68 parking lot.

I-68 bridge downstream | Upstream from park towards US 40

Moving north from the River Road bridge, the steep hills to the west push the shaded road close to the river. The protective band of vegetation is not thick, with minimal bush and vine undergrowth making it easy to approach the river. The eastern bank borders open fields and the rural noises of farming and cattle mixes with the nose-nipping aroma of manure to complete the picture. Once on the river, do not be fooled by the shallow appearance. The water is crystal clear and runs deeper than it looks. The secret to success on the Casselman is to find the deep cuts and protected structure. Do not ignore the banks, since the big fish huddle near cover, causing experts to advise anglers not enter the river at all since the fish tend spook on the sound of gentle splashing. There are no rushing rapids to conceal your approach since the gradient is flat and gentle.

At 39.70776,-79.12589, the road briefly touches the river and is the last place to walk to the shore until the road winds its way through a farm and returns to the river at 39.71469,-79.12332. Start fishing at any of the obvious parking areas with the last one being adjacent to a path at 39.716144,-79.120648 where the road veers left and a large field becomes an insurmountable protective cushion of private property. The river deepens at this location and it may be problematic to wade depending on the water levels. According to the DNR, flows lower than 150 CFS on the Casselman River gage at Grantsville are optimum for fishing.

The Casselman River is the body of water that receives more trout than any other in the entire State. It is number one in terms of stocking with over 9,100 fish inserted in the spring.

Savage River

Approximate Boundary: 39.481189,-79.067967 to 39.584491,-79.091957 (9.77 miles)

Type: Varies

Directions:
North: From I-68, take exit 24 onto Avilton Lonaconing Road. Turn right onto Lower New Germany Road heading south. Turn left onto Twin Churches Road. It becomes Westernport Road. Turn right onto Savage River Road and follow it to the junction with Poplar Lick. This is the northern boundary of the stocked section.

South: From Westernport, drive west on MD 135/Pratt Street. Turn right on Savage River Road. Follow it approximately 0.3 miles to the first turnout on the right that provides access to the Trophy Area.

The Savage River is the centerpiece of the 54,000 acre Savage River State Forest with the Potomac State Forest providing an additional buffer of public land at the lower boundary near the reservoir. Beyond the great fishing on the Savage River, nearly every tributary feeding into the Savage River Reservoir supports wild brook trout. I discuss the ones that are well-known elsewhere in the book. However, if you are resourceful and have access to a topographic map, you can venture off to discover your own wild brook trout wonderland by following almost any "blue line". If you intend to spend the night, be sure to obtain a backpack camping permit after self-registering at one of the six sites scattered throughout the property.

The Savage River Reservoir provides a geographically massive, recognizable breakpoint between the special regulation areas below the dam and the general fishing available on the mainstem of the river. There are three distinct fishing sections. Above the dam, the mainstem of the river from Poplar Lick down to the lake operates under normal "put and take" regulations and the DNR stocks it heavily during the season. It ranks number four in overall numbers of fish. Below the dam, the first mile is fly fishing only followed by trophy trout water (artificial lures and flies only) extending to the town of Bloomington. If you fish with spin gear, do not encroach upon the fly fishing section since you will surely be reported by another angler.

The common environmental theme below the dam is "snot slick" rocks. If you do not use a wading staff, you will surely die if you try and fish without that advantage. The boulders were tailor-made to snap ankles and trip anglers who, to the sadistic enjoyment of their fishing buddies, will flail desperately in four dimensions, rod flying, only to splat unceremoniously upon the rocks. Exercise extreme caution and be sure of your footing to remain safe. As you can imagine, those same boulders channel the fast-moving water into an infinite number of deep cuts, creating plunge pools to shelter crafty, lurking monster browns and a smaller number of nimble brookies. The banks are not friendly and restrict movement.

Throughout its entire length, the Savage River runs clear and clean over a trout compatible rocky bottom with a typical width of 30 to 50 feet. Where the gradient picks up below the dam, the habitat becomes even better. During the period when the Savage River Reservoir was undergoing repairs,

anglers across the State were concerned that the two foot deep blanket of silt dumped do'
from the reservoir would destroy this pristine fishery. Thankfully, torrential rainfall
reservoir and allowed the management to celebrate completion with an aggressive, violent 4,500 cis
flush. According to the DNR, it cleared out almost all of the sediment with the positive effect of adding
clean spawning gravel from the bottom of the reservoir. Granted, the trout population suffered a 19%
reduction, but there are still over 800 trout per mile and, hopefully, the density will bounce back to
the near record level of 1,716 trout per mile measured in 2008 (FFO section). The vibrant insect life
that spurs trout health and growth continued uninterrupted during the repair.

Trophy Area

Approximate Boundary: 39.481255,-79.068017 to 39.501027,-79.114514 (3.71 miles)
DNR Guidance: Mainstem from its mouth upstream for a distance of approximately 2.7 miles to the
lower suspension bridge.

Type: Artificial Lures Only

Access Point: Various turnouts along Savage River Road to include: 39.50155,-79.10718 (lower
suspension bridge), 39.49573,-79.10236, 39.49642,-79.09863, 39.49283,-79.09818 (fish upstream
only), 39.49057,-79.09553 (may be posted soon), 39.49118,-79.09156 (fish downstream only),
39.48804,-79.08677 (200 feet from river), 39.48729,-79.08578 (150 feet from river), 39.48659,-
79.08464 (west of first bridge), 39.48625,-79.08248 (at first bridge), 39.48308,-79.07369 (first
turnout near Bloomington)

The easiest wading in the trophy area is near Bloomington. Moving upstream from the town, the first
two turnouts provide the best access with the one at the bridge being preferred. The first turnout
north from Bloomington sits on a high ridge approximately 50 feet above the streambed. The pitch is
acute down the steep hill, so devise an exit strategy before entering the river. Access at the bridge is
as easy as the first spot is hard. The best approach to fishing downstream is to enter along the
southern bank and stay between the large ridge that parallels the river and the water's edge.

It is fully overgrown with vegetation, so walk as far downstream as you can using the narrow gap
between the rhododendrons and the rock ridge and then fish up to the bridge while remaining in the
river. Fair warning. Aaron Run joins the Savage River near the bridge and is subject to acid drainage
from old mines farther up the mountainside. Depending on the effectiveness of the acid mine
drainage mitigation efforts that include the installation of lime dozers similar to those on the North
Branch of the Potomac, there may be fewer trout downstream than upstream from this point.

Savage River
Regulations and property ownership may have changed since publication.
It is your responsibility to know and obey all regulations and not trespass on private property.
129

At first access point below the bridge   Upstream from first access point

Above the bridge, while there are numerous turnouts, you may encounter "posted" water. Be consciously aware of private property as you fish from those locations. Between the lower suspension bridge marking the upstream boundary of the trophy area and the transition into the fly fishing only section, the river drops almost 300 feet as it plunges towards that first turnout above Bloomington. This creates fast water, deeply cut channels and challenging pools as the river surges to reach a width of over 50 feet. Anglers can spend the entire day working a 50 yard stretch if they cover all of the water.

The water is deceptive and what appears to be shallow may actually be a deep channel. The clarity causes everything to appear unproductively shallow but, in reality, there is no dirt or muck floating in the crystal-clear water to provide an indication of depth. Each boulder shelters holding positions. This is the zone for highly technical fishing that gives the advantage to a fly angler since a spinner takes a certain amount of distance to activate once the retrieve starts.

Anglers can get a bird's eye view of the good spots from the road. On a weekend, grab the first place you see since the exceptional fishing attracts an early crowd. Those who drive the complete distance up to the dam to check out the entire river may not be able to find a parking spot on the way back down.

Fly Fishing Only Area

Approximate Boundary: 39.506491,-79.132683 to 39.501027,-79.114514 (1.18 miles)
DNR Guidance: Savage River mainstem from the Savage River Reservoir Dam downstream to the lower suspension bridge (Allegany Bridge).

Type: Fly Fishing Only

Access Point:
- Lower suspension bridge (39.50155,-79.10718)
- Upper suspension bridge (39.50117,-79.11443)
- Second bridge (39.50268,-79.12426)

Beyond the restriction on the type of tackle, the key difference between the fly fishing only section and the trophy area is the higher gradient as the river drops 157 feet in this short distance. The gradient increases the crush of the water as it charges downstream desperately looking for the first place to level out and lose energy. Large boulders speckle the landscape, all densely populated with flyrodders in search of the massive fish that call this part of the river home. In fact, it is worth taking up fly fishing just to fish here! Narrower than downstream, but with more deep channels and even deeper pools, the indigenous fish are highly educated since most fly anglers are catch and releasers.

While many believe that the best fly to use is a nymph, the big fish look for a more substantial meal and that gives the edge to streamers. However, given the rocky bottom and the robust hatches, dry fly fishing can be fantastic at the right time. Since the fish are wary, old-timers caution that 7X tippet is required to achieve the appropriately deceptive drag free drift. Others claim that you can be successful using 6X for dries and nymphs and even 5X for streamers. Who knows? Use what works. One final challenge is the thick accumulation of algae on every rock. If fishing with nymphs, they will come up covered in slime on every cast unless you tune either the indicator or the split shot to keep the nymph floating freely over the bottom. This is one of the reasons why many prefer dancing dry flies delicately across the surface.

Fly fishing only on a misty morning

Upstream from bridge

Mainstem

Approximate Boundary: 39.539131,-79.13764 to 39.586376,-79.09215 (4.88 miles)
DNR Guidance: Mainstem from Savage Reservoir upstream to Poplar Lick.

Type: Put and Take

Access Point: There are 17 different turnouts along Savage River Road between the upper end of the reservoir and the confluence of Poplar Lick.

As a general statement, turn out and park near the confluence of any tributary stream to find the largest pools and the best fishing. The mainstem of the Savage is the fourth most heavily stocked river in Maryland and received 8,185 fish in the spring of 2011. The almost five miles of fishable length above the reservoir argues for the continued insertion of large numbers of fish. In fact, it is a shame that the DNR can't move all the trout they stock in Deep Creek Lake where they instantly disappear into the depths of that massive body of water to the Savage where we have a better shot at catching them.

The river easily supports trout with a rocky bottom and widths that can be up to 60 feet. It is deeper on the mainstem than downstream, but not deep enough to keep the average sized angler from wading at normal water levels. The river runs through a fairly level valley, losing only a little over 200 feet between the start of the stocked section and the reservoir. Although the water moves quickly, it is not oppressively fast. In addition, the cold water algae that grows with abandon below the reservoir is not a problem here. Every bend in the river hides a deep pool and the best producing locations are close to the road where the stock truck has easy access to insert fish. Even then, the river runs deep enough that the fish distribute themselves pretty well across the length within 10 days of the stocking. As I discussed in the fish behavior chapter, most stocked fish move downstream and that should inform your fishing strategy. Start at the lower end and work upstream.

While the trophy sections downstream of the reservoir demanded highly technical, almost expert level skills, the mainstem is ideal for the novice angler while still being scenic enough to bring joy to the heart of anyone who values catching fish in an idyllic setting. With the exception of the few residential areas scattered along the river, there is minimal evidence of humans to reinforce a remote feel. Thankfully, people routinely pick up their trash and keep the Savage looking good.

Weekend campers find plenty of options adjacent to the river with a large camping area in Big Run State Park at the northern end of the reservoir. For those who prefer camping in a more natural mountain setting, take advantage of any of the campsites along Westernport Road (Elk Lick - 6 sites) or Big Run Road (21 sites). Although the maps show campsites along the Poplar Lick off-road vehicle (ORV) trail, the DNR permanently closed that trail to vehicles – hikers are still welcome.

The mainstem of the Savage is the third most heavily stocked stream in the state.

Youghiogheny River

Oakland

Approximate Boundary: 39.387188,-79.461551 to 39.500332,-79.415889 (12.63 miles)
DNR Guidance: Mainstem upstream of the junction of Muddy Creek.

Type: Put and Take

Directions:
To go to the south end, follow MD 39 west from Oakland. Turn left onto Ottobein Street. Ottobein becomes Kendall Drive. Turn right on Crellin Underwood Road.

To go to the north end, turn west onto S Center Street from US 219 in the center of Oakland. Continue onto N Bradley Lane. Turn right on Liberty Street. Liberty becomes Herrington Manor Road. Turn right onto Swallow Falls Road. Park on the east side of the bridge over the river.

Access Point:
- Parking area on the east side of Crellin Underwood Road north of the junction of Snowy Creek with the river (39.38778,-79.463742)
- Parking lot of the baseball field just south of Snowy Creek (39.38606,-79.462529)
- Junction of MD 39 and Ottobein Street (39.391039,-79.463801)
- Bridge crossing on Liberty Street (39.424158,-79.421808)
- Bridge crossing at Swallow Falls Road (39.494247,-79.416273)

Unless you fish from a canoe or kayak with a greater interest in paddling than fishing, do not become elated at the prospect of over 12 miles of stocked water. There are only a few accessible points for kayakers, the stock truck or wading anglers. Moving west, away from Oakland, the worse it becomes. At the start of the stocked section in the tiny village of Crellin, the river is a muddy, silty mess with little to recommend it. The river is wide and shallow consisting of high banks with scattered trees throwing some shade over the water. Since the river runs through town, a mix of residential and industrial buildings peppers the banks conspiring to create an unfriendly, unattractive vista. In short, not a compelling or pleasant fishing location.

Thankfully, by the time the river reaches the Liberty Street bridge crossing miles downstream, it is dramatically different. The bottom is now uniformly coated with a layer of rock with large boulders providing random points of interest, creating pools and holding locations. Access the river via the fisherman's trail on the west side of the bridge. Rocks and boulders line the banks and hold back the vegetation. There are still plenty of trees to provide interesting scenery as well as a little bit of shade.

Liberty Street bridge upstream | Liberty Street bridge downstream

The next access point is at the Swallow Falls State Park. There is a small turnout, outside of the park (no fee), on the east side of the bridge. Only a fool would wade in the river downstream since Swallow Falls is only a short distance away. There is a trail leading from the parking lot to the north side of the bridge providing access to the upstream river. However, unless you are willing to walk over a mile, be prepared for a total waste of time. Upstream of the bridge, the river bottom consists primarily of a slick, flat rock shelf that holds no structure and prevents the creation of pools or the generation of forage to attract fish. In the far distance, you can see some large boulders poking up out of the streambed and those mark the first place where the fishing becomes acceptable. The flat shelf continues upstream until 39.486957,-79.408566 where rocks and pools take control.

Swallow Falls upstream | Swallow Falls downstream

If you walk across the street from the parking lot, follow the trail down the east side of the river to get a bird's eye view of Swallow Falls and fish the downstream river outside of the danger zone. Exercise extreme caution if you choose this option and wear a PFD.

The Oakland section is the 25th most heavily stocked stream in the State.

Hoyes Run - Sang Run

Approximate Boundary: 39.565967,-79.429372 to 39.52427,-79.414551 (3.71 miles)
DNR Guidance: Mainstem beginning at a red post approximately 100 yards upstream of the Deep Creek Lake tailrace and extending downstream four miles to the Sang Run Bridge.

Type: Catch and Return - Artificial Lures

Directions:
- Hoyes Run: From I-68 take Exit 14 for MD 219 South. Turn right on Sang Run Road. Turn left on Hoyes Run Road. Turn right on Oakland-Sang Run Road. The parking area is across the bridge.
- Sang Run: From I-68, take exit 4 for MD 42S near Friendsville. Turn right on Bischoff Road followed by another right on Sang Run Road about two miles later. Follow Sang Run Road to the parking area a couple hundred yards up from the bridge.

Access Point:
- Sang Run parking lot off of Sang Run Road near the bridge (39.565574,-79.426642)
- Hoyes Run kiosk parking lot 200 feet west of the intersection of Hoyes Run Road and Oakland Sang Run Road (39.529344,-79.41025)

This section of the Youghiogheny River is popular with anglers as a result of the catch and return regulations that contribute to trout densities of over 1,000 trout per mile near Hoyes Run with the lower Sang Run area holding 500 trout per mile. A good number of these brown and rainbow trout measure over 20 inches long. In addition, the recurring rush of water from the Deep Creek power plant, to include special summer releases to maintain the cold water habitat, provides a continual churn and refresh of the food that makes it an attractive place for trout.

Hoyes Run

Hoyes Run

This is big water. In most places, the river runs 100 feet wide with plenty of slick rocks and oddly sized boulders making wading a challenge. For those who fished the North Branch or the Savage, wading is not as rough as either of those rivers. As a result of the width, there is no perception of pressure even when other anglers are on the river. The dramatic panorama of forested mountains merging into clean, clear water makes this a "must do" fishing experience. Since the river only drops 300 feet between Hoyes Run and Sang Run, it is low gradient without any exciting drops to produce the deep plunge pools or dramatic waterfalls present at Swallow Falls. In fact, the whitewater kayak crowd skips over this stretch in their description of the river and writes it off as "flat water." Their preference is for the adrenaline producing, human bending, and kayak destroying washing machines that fleck the river from Swallow Falls to the power plant just south of the Hoyes Run access and again from Sang Run down to Friendsville - both include class IV-V rapids.

Since there are no plunge pools, look for channels and pools carved between large boulders. Be alert for random depths that may be over your head since there is no standard size. The river is easily wadeable, just exercise caution and be aware of the surroundings.

Obviously, when the release from the power plant is underway, river levels rise dramatically depending on whether it is a regular or special whitewater release. The water level can go up a foot or two and that brings up a key point of caution. When fishing, do not become so enthralled with what your lure or fly is doing that you ignore what is happening around you. Periodically look upstream and mark the water level against a prominent landmark. As soon as you see that landmark start to disappear, move immediately to the eastern bank since that is where you parked your vehicle. In general, releases occur Monday, Friday and Saturday between 11 AM and 2 PM. Although releases can occur at any time, you should call Deep Creek Hydro at 508-251-7704 for the release schedule. Many anglers use the release schedule to their advantage since the fishing picks up after the churning water stirs up food. To exploit the release, start the day at Sang Run and when the release becomes noticeable, drive to Hoyes Run to fish downstream in its wake.

Sang Run

Sang Run

If you are adventurous, you can follow the trail that connects the two parking lots on the east side of the river to move away from the pressure near the parking lot. There are no other access points off of Oakland Sang Run Road even though it connects Hoyes Run with Sang Run as it runs along the high ridgeline bordering the east bank of the river.

Friendsville (Put and Take)

Approximate Boundary: 39.659165,-79.409101 to 39.664811,-79.407126 (2,322 feet)
DNR Guidance: Upstream side of the MD 42 bridge downstream 0.4 miles to a site 50 yards downstream of Maple Street (at confluence of Minnow Run).

Type: Put and Take

Directions:
From I-68, take exit 4. If eastbound, merge onto MD 42 and turn left onto 1st Avenue and follow it into town. If westbound, turn right on Maple Street and follow it into town.

Access Point:
- Street parking on Chestnut Street (39.662934,-79.406832)
- Under the I-68 bridge on Water Street (39.661148,-79.40886)

There is not much to the put and take section adjacent to Friendsville. This short stretch sits on the west side of town hemmed in by residential property. Access from the east is available by using the trail to the historic town of Kendall adjacent to the intersection of Oak Street and Morris Avenue. The trail runs for two miles along the river as it follows the former Oakland-Confluence narrow gauge railroad bed. Recognize that upstream of the bridge supporting MD 42, no stocking occurs, so anything in that direction is wild.

To use this access point, park in town and walk to the start of the trail. If you like to fish using a bike, this is a perfect place to do that. Bike from spot to spot to cover the most river possible. Be sure you are out by sunset since the area closes at that time. No camping! As a side note, the trail provides access to the rough part of the river enjoyed by the kayaking crowd. The rapids have dangerous sounding names like Luke's Final Insult, Double Pencil Sharpener, Wrights Hole, with the Meat Cleaver being about a mile upstream of Kendall. Each of these is associated with dramatic plunges and the associated pools that can produce good fishing. If you venture this far upstream in search of the whitewater, be absolutely sure of your footing and where a PFD.

Trail to Kendall

Downstream towards I-68

Pulling back from the adrenaline associated with Class V rapids to the real world in the designated "put and take" section, options to park are limited. Water Street parallels the western bank of the river, but the shoulder is even more constricted than on the east side. Signs cautioning anglers not to park in this congested area dot the landscape. Continue south on Water Street and park underneath the I-68 bridge.

By the time the river reaches Friendsville, it runs wide and flat. The bottom consists of small to medium sized rocks and boulders. There is a small drop in gradient at the south end of town that creates a set of riffles, but nothing else to attract attention. The east side is usually deeper than the west side, but there are a few deep spots on the west in the short distance between the two bridges.

Friendsville (Delayed Harvest)

Approximate Boundary: 39.664811,-79.407126 to 39.674229,-79.391264 (1.8 miles)
DNR Guidance: Below Friendsville from site 50 yards downstream of Maple Street (at the confluence of Minnow Run) downstream to the gas-line crossing upstream of Youghiogheny Reservoir.

Type: Delayed Harvest

Directions:
East: From I-68, take exit 4. Turn right on Maple Street. Turn left on 2nd Avenue. Turn into the Friendsville Community Park using Old River Road.

South: From I-68, take exit 4 to merge onto MD 42. Turn left onto 1st Avenue. Turn right onto Park Street. Turn left onto 2nd Avenue. Use Old River Road to enter the Friendsville Community Park.

Access Point:
- Friendsville Community Park boat launch (39.66844,-79.398972)
- Various turnouts on the dirt track that parallels the river with the main ones being at 39.67419,-79.39071, 39.67262,-79.39059, 39.66886,-79.39104, 39.66686,-79.39315

In addition to catching trout, you can also pick up walleye and smallmouth bass, making this a year-round fishing destination. Although the delayed harvest section starts north of Maple Street at the west edge of town, private property borders the river until it runs adjacent to the Friendsville Community Park. There is plenty of easy access, to include a canoe launch, from the park. In addition, you can drive east on the dirt road through the South Selbysport Access Area to continue downriver.

The two choices for fishing are driven by the presence of the large island dividing the river at the east end of the park. Unless you are willing to walk or drive another 1,500 feet to the east to rejoin the mainstem of the river, a quick, good option is to begin fishing in either direction from the park itself.

To move downstream, leverage the access the Corps of Engineers granted Maryland and bump down the dirt road all the way to the end. As you drive, observe the river to the left and pick your spot carefully. Initially, the bank is treacherously high, making the descent to the river's edge problematic. Eventually, the road edges closer to the river and access is not an issue. The river continues to offer up ideal fish holding structure. While the amount of sand grows the farther downstream the river runs, there are still plenty of rocks and boulders clogging the riverbed.

The dramatic width of several hundred feet adds to the excitement since it is impossible to feel pressured on a river this large. At normal water levels, the current runs slow. However, the high water marks staining the trees confirm that the river routinely overflows its banks and turns the road into a muddy mess that may be difficult for vehicles without four-wheel-drive to traverse. Those high water marks also scream caution – wear a PFD! If you decide to stop at one of the small turnoffs chipped out of the rocky hill, be sure to leave the road open to allow others to pass. In fact, do not bother to park and fish until you are beyond the tip of the large island (39.66686,-79.39315) that divides the river unless you really want to fish the sideshow instead of the mainstem.

For those who like to fish using a canoe or kayak, there is an informal put-in/take-out at the power line easement that is only about a mile downstream from the canoe launch in the park. If you have a bike, you can do a self-shuttle. Leave your bike at the take-out and use it to ride back to your vehicle when done fishing.

Water Flow (cfs)

Barnum Gage Flow

	Mean of daily mean values for each day for 24 years of record in cfs											
Day	Jan	Feb	Mar	Apr	May	Jun	Jul	Aug	Sep	Oct	Nov	Dec
1	876	637	887	977	669	728	253	199	178	277	302	563
2	718	658	869	1,150	599	615	218	217	166	291	312	523
3	689	696	1,030	953	613	474	645	188	164	298	382	535
4	797	635	1,180	1,120	704	483	452	211	186	241	335	574
5	867	539	1,290	1,200	653	498	390	208	203	258	332	537
6	755	531	1,440	1,050	610	538	318	186	298	335	335	536
7	662	514	1,250	981	717	504	270	204	250	374	368	714
8	646	487	983	919	713	449	277	191	215	314	595	794
9	601	471	858	952	717	384	317	161	189	568	477	994
10	671	449	812	879	600	410	324	203	165	547	409	793
11	696	559	749	768	554	419	367	177	178	453	385	736
12	647	540	774	718	559	492	301	195	204	350	386	673
13	542	541	1,070	900	674	455	289	190	239	298	416	654
14	579	619	1,070	814	607	484	241	216	306	266	429	645
15	540	548	1,130	849	635	446	214	244	252	228	426	616
16	453	628	1,040	833	693	434	195	322	204	229	425	581
17	441	678	1,130	764	623	340	190	245	188	229	407	546
18	444	694	1,010	699	606	358	171	415	176	298	403	512
19	462	669	961	636	573	326	170	385	195	236	413	495
20	468	690	1,050	605	549	313	179	280	188	234	465	519
21	493	751	1,260	560	587	302	187	220	207	255	392	683
22	473	807	1,280	553	512	340	172	195	222	229	363	896
23	434	887	1,140	700	533	496	185	290	224	202	379	823
24	463	1,070	1,070	936	701	403	189	263	220	248	431	705
25	528	1,150	1,090	982	640	304	172	211	196	295	463	804
26	688	1,170	1,070	791	516	312	193	201	204	333	428	768
27	632	1,010	1,030	799	480	295	173	225	199	278	418	720
28	577	872	1,090	761	482	338	172	195	232	274	471	616
29	740	1,020	1,030	730	491	354	210	177	238	317	511	604
30	754		940	741	526	266	179	165	220	284	524	626
31	664		997		567		195	167		295		654
Avg	613	684	1,051	844	603	419	252	224	210	301	413	659

Kitzmiller Gage Flow

Mean of daily mean values for each day for 41 years of record in cfs												
Day	Jan	Feb	Mar	Apr	May	Jun	Jul	Aug	Sep	Oct	Nov	Dec
1	630	752	874	792	693	457	191	150	90	155	241	431
2	622	721	880	958	566	444	154	144	96	157	245	377
3	694	691	914	911	594	413	385	141	101	154	266	441
4	700	596	1,060	1,010	578	504	315	172	110	125	263	524
5	678	572	1,490	1,010	560	460	266	212	111	140	267	433
6	610	662	1,290	919	570	415	258	267	173	170	242	463
7	607	722	1,070	933	618	343	203	166	144	213	261	600
8	516	582	915	879	633	338	209	151	150	172	360	672
9	481	574	817	894	593	287	250	129	137	291	305	725
10	613	626	773	822	533	329	251	166	99	285	310	633
11	598	682	804	715	502	420	233	132	109	222	293	630
12	536	603	892	720	548	363	202	198	135	183	343	598
13	467	609	1,080	778	580	484	185	273	149	169	278	594
14	500	727	1,070	759	550	478	153	210	162	144	264	570
15	601	683	1,030	827	566	321	188	163	125	345	263	511
16	531	598	937	786	626	322	157	205	106	250	296	466
17	436	599	943	708	526	271	136	178	96	178	289	413
18	451	660	816	641	509	305	120	575	118	196	273	437
19	436	663	940	579	496	272	129	274	103	159	306	430
20	407	606	1,100	563	533	242	140	196	101	153	321	427
21	475	737	1,180	528	502	228	144	243	121	174	300	532
22	490	699	1,120	606	430	250	137	167	159	148	304	623
23	567	793	969	657	430	325	148	183	136	155	264	605
24	594	957	1,040	816	519	270	154	132	114	235	323	577
25	559	1,000	1,010	799	461	292	132	110	94	215	318	621
26	639	907	967	777	364	269	125	135	93	215	313	624
27	608	777	952	768	430	214	137	125	95	215	287	576
28	562	702	1,040	784	513	206	136	110	126	213	391	487
29	698	664	1,070	804	429	216	177	100	124	259	540	566
30	764		979	738	415	184	121	85	106	242	462	608
31	664		877		543		122	89		252		621
Avg	572	672	997	783	529	331	183	180	119	199	306	542

Steyer Gage Flow:

Day	\multicolumn{12}{c}{Mean of daily mean values for each day for 52 years of record in, cfs}
Day	Jan	Feb	Mar	Apr	May	Jun	Jul	Aug	Sep	Oct	Nov	Dec
1	262	210	275	303	239	153	88	89	53	58	86	196
2	242	205	315	333	198	151	81	74	61	64	97	189
3	249	221	304	302	195	142	158	75	55	58	101	181
4	237	214	364	347	214	146	109	83	94	50	142	187
5	249	187	503	335	248	147	104	117	60	57	189	185
6	228	207	481	305	252	157	105	159	112	61	126	168
7	245	204	380	311	245	143	72	80	76	83	131	237
8	228	202	332	294	259	121	107	82	62	60	147	224
9	217	289	306	295	240	128	127	80	49	106	131	252
10	262	281	299	292	206	128	141	82	43	97	142	228
11	212	252	278	283	194	154	150	80	54	74	130	231
12	212	210	308	266	189	127	119	136	61	63	154	219
13	210	211	343	295	195	130	110	107	60	60	120	219
14	220	269	336	265	204	150	92	88	78	53	115	228
15	247	264	353	292	191	117	80	75	59	49	114	206
16	205	249	304	301	194	129	83	92	51	56	128	195
17	176	237	308	270	177	111	72	81	65	58	124	182
18	189	262	292	234	199	113	70	101	67	67	128	192
19	270	327	339	233	207	94	119	80	109	67	139	186
20	220	283	385	222	184	107	108	75	60	69	146	215
21	199	281	423	213	163	103	80	83	55	93	126	230
22	214	266	385	247	151	103	88	67	52	75	132	252
23	265	316	335	238	148	142	85	84	61	83	125	251
24	259	357	356	271	192	110	97	61	50	91	139	238
25	248	341	337	261	166	103	73	51	50	79	139	258
26	245	323	346	261	180	87	111	46	58	77	157	256
27	214	272	316	244	161	83	130	60	57	81	154	214
28	204	262	312	250	156	88	99	53	66	80	226	185
29	273	296	337	251	170	88	129	48	61	94	222	202
30	251		337	241	155	80	87	46	50	88	193	204
31	235		310		191		102	47		90		239
Avg	232	250	342	275	196	121	102	80	63	72	140	214

Mount Storm (Stony River) Gage

	Mean of daily mean values for each day for 46 years of record in cfs											
Day	Jan	Feb	Mar	Apr	May	Jun	Jul	Aug	Sep	Oct	Nov	Dec
1	131	102	155	193	135	106	44	40	20	54	51	111
2	139	107	157	199	116	88	40	36	23	41	54	99
3	138	109	194	172	119	93	98	36	24	34	59	85
4	135	118	215	183	140	108	87	38	54	29	66	91
5	139	118	251	172	142	96	62	29	45	33	270	92
6	128	106	258	162	178	96	51	42	114	35	130	89
7	127	106	225	194	140	89	44	29	99	38	109	99
8	122	100	195	165	150	75	55	28	57	49	158	104
9	131	165	191	183	122	74	66	29	43	66	101	110
10	112	112	185	178	128	74	60	29	29	73	103	104
11	114	118	162	174	118	75	61	29	23	60	83	108
12	101	103	165	184	101	70	44	43	22	42	86	111
13	96	104	202	166	97	87	48	71	22	39	76	109
14	91	137	215	149	107	96	38	53	26	31	68	107
15	98	158	235	167	117	50	36	39	27	30	65	99
16	112	120	200	194	127	59	37	42	33	33	67	105
17	99	119	218	170	109	58	40	37	45	34	70	103
18	98	132	223	154	122	58	36	43	52	41	73	108
19	141	177	249	146	136	49	46	39	77	41	70	96
20	124	135	272	146	113	50	42	35	37	40	75	97
21	94	142	271	128	113	53	38	40	43	50	72	97
22	91	159	245	136	101	52	37	31	41	42	73	107
23	98	179	240	142	92	61	36	36	36	45	67	118
24	97	233	254	152	104	57	36	29	32	56	71	117
25	110	173	261	134	102	59	31	26	32	53	61	133
26	125	176	243	124	108	48	35	24	34	50	62	118
27	121	164	272	124	111	41	55	26	34	49	66	89
28	108	153	237	129	98	44	42	25	39	48	107	84
29	95	162	229	137	116	42	44	26	41	56	98	95
30	102		203	136	102	40	38	23	42	55	108	108
31	109		186		130		50	23		56		110
Avg	114	133	220	160	119	68	48	35	42	45	87	103

Gage Height

Barnum Gage Height:

Monthly mean in ft (Calculation Period: 1973-10-01 -> 1978-01-30)												
Year	Jan	Feb	Mar	Apr	May	Jun	Jul	Aug	Sep	Oct	Nov	Dec
1973										3.14	3.50	3.97
1974	4.49	3.81	3.84	4.14	4.30	4.47		2.56	2.86			
1975	4.01	4.59	4.14	3.78	4.04	3.19	2.75	3.26	3.41	3.46	3.02	3.20
1976	4.35		3.74	4.09	1.55	2.66	2.63	2.39	2.35	4.02	3.53	3.66
1977	3.20	4.22	5.60	3.99	3.07	2.74	2.50	2.57	2.29	2.82	4.01	4.15
1978	3.43											
Avg	3.89	4.21	4.33	4.00	3.24	3.27	2.62	2.69	2.73	3.36	3.51	3.74

Kitzmiller Gage Height:

Gage Height - Monthly mean in ft (Calculation Period: 1974-02-01 -> 1978-02-30)												
Year	Jan	Feb	Mar	Apr	May	Jun	Jul	Aug	Sep	Oct	Nov	Dec
1974		4.11	4.30	4.48	3.74	4.54	3.34	2.79	2.97	2.79	3.10	4.17
1975	4.63	4.98	4.77	4.32	4.46	3.29	2.97	3.70	3.74	3.76	3.19	3.51
1976	4.49	4.65	4.09	3.72	3.36	3.58	2.98	2.63	2.58	4.56	3.86	3.85
1977	3.44	4.15	5.01	4.19	3.12	2.99	2.72	2.83	2.51	3.15	4.39	4.52
1978	4.06	3.91										
Avg	4.16	4.36	4.54	4.18	3.67	3.60	3.00	2.99	2.95	3.57	3.63	4.01

Steyer Gage Height:

Monthly mean in ft (Calculation Period: 1973-11-01 -> 2007-09-30)												
Year	Jan	Feb	Mar	Apr	May	Jun	Jul	Aug	Sep	Oct	Nov	Dec
1973											3.05	3.26
1974		3.18	3.12	3.26	2.90	3.73	2.42	2.36	2.53	2.34	2.69	3.44
1975	3.43	3.42	3.30	3.17	3.15	2.68	2.41	2.78	2.67	2.68	2.61	2.88
1976	3.34	3.39	3.04	2.82	2.62	2.80	2.50	2.31	2.27	3.27	2.87	3.02
1977	2.93	3.53	3.52	3.01	2.63	2.50	2.40	2.51	2.30	2.71	3.16	3.31
1978	3.25											
2001										2.11	2.04	2.31
2002	2.61	2.58	2.87	3.21	3.11	2.52	2.81	2.35	2.21	2.48	2.92	2.84
2003	2.97	2.86	3.50	3.07	3.01	3.12	2.75	2.75	3.36	2.68	3.11	2.94
2004	3.04	3.02	3.40	3.10	2.70	2.77	2.40	2.32	2.38	2.40	2.86	2.93
2005	3.06	2.96	3.14	2.91	2.79	2.45	2.56	2.26	2.08	2.23	2.62	2.82
2006	3.20	2.72	2.68	2.97	2.61	2.60	2.45	2.18	2.20	2.44	2.65	2.44
2007	2.82	2.81	3.41	2.95	2.46	2.20	2.47	2.61	2.17			
Avg	3.07	3.05	3.20	3.05	2.80	2.74	2.52	2.44	2.42	2.53	2.78	2.93

Mount Storm (Stony River) Gage Height

Monthly mean in ft (Calculation Period: 2003-06-01 -> 2007-09-30)												
Year	Jan	Feb	Mar	Apr	May	Jun	Jul	Aug	Sep	Oct	Nov	Dec
2003						3.07	2.33	2.54	3.35	2.41	3.13	2.92
2004	2.76	2.87	3.61	3.37	2.86	2.44	2.21	1.95	2.91	2.39	2.90	2.84
2005	2.91	2.79	3.20	2.95	2.79	2.05	2.31	1.98	1.66	1.84	2.18	2.69
2006	3.35	2.59	2.57	2.86	2.48	2.28	2.15	1.62	1.94	2.39	2.85	2.25
2007	2.77	2.51	3.75	3.16	2.34	1.82	2.01	2.00	1.68			
Avg	2.95	2.69	3.28	3.08	2.62	2.33	2.20	2.02	2.31	2.25	2.76	2.60

Water Temperature

This is only available, even partially, for a few gages.

Barnum Temperature:

Monthly mean in deg C and deg F (Calculation Period: 1980-07-01 -> 1985-10-30)												
Year	Jan	Feb	Mar	Apr	May	Jun	Jul	Aug	Sep	Oct	Nov	Dec
1980							25.1	31.1	18.7	12.7	3.1	4.3
1981		4.6	3.7	10.1	16.6	18.7	22.6		15.6	12.7	8.0	4.2
1982	2.0	2.2	4.2	6.6	11.4	14.8	18.3	19.4	18.3	13.6	9.0	8.2
1983	4.8	3.8	5.4	6.8	11.0	16.5	17.3	16.9	16.5	13.7	8.4	5.5
1984	2.9	3.3	3.5	6.2	11.1	14.6	15.8	16.0	16.2	14.2	8.9	6.6
1985	4.8	3.1	4.7	7.7	14.6	16.7	17.7	18.5	17.5	15.0		
Avg C	3.6	3.4	4.3	7.5	13.0	16.2	19.4	20.4	17.1	13.7	7.5	5.8
Avg F	38.5	38.1	39.7	45.5	55.4	61.2	66.9	68.7	62.8	56.7	45.5	42.4

Kitzmiller Temperature:

I recommend you not rely too much on the official Kitzmiller view since it is only based on one year of data. I pulled down the raw data and used it to calculate a broader view.

Only official available data from USGS:

Monthly mean in deg C and deg F (Calculation Period: 1993-10-01 -> 1994-09-30)												
	Jan	Feb	Mar	Apr	May	Jun	Jul	Aug	Sep	Oct	Nov	Dec
C	3.1	2.8	11.1	11.2	13.1	24.7	21.7	20.7	16.9	11.3	5.8	3.6
F	37.6	37.0	52.0	52.2	55.6	76.5	71.1	69.3	62.4	52.3	42.4	38.5

Detailed look I calculated using daily data between 2002 and 2006:

Mean of daily values for each day for 5 years of record											
Day	**Jan**	**Feb**	**Mar**	**Apr**	**May**	**Jun**	**Jul**	**Aug**	**Sep**	**Oct**	**Nov**	**Dec**
1	42.4	36.9	38.4	49.1	58.3	65.8	71.4	77.9	67.5	60.3	51.0	42.9
2	42.8	35.9	36.9	49.4	59.3	64.9	72.3	76.6	67.1	62.7	49.7	38.7
3	44.9	36.1	36.4	48.8	55.0	61.3	72.4	76.0	67.4	63.7	48.2	36.2
4	46.4	35.7	36.1	46.8	54.0	61.4	73.0	75.1	68.0	61.5	47.1	36.2
5	46.0	34.2	37.9	45.4	54.9	62.9	72.4	74.0	68.1	60.9	47.5	36.1
6	44.4	33.7	39.4	46.0	57.2	63.6	71.9	72.3	65.9	58.8	48.8	36.1
7	39.2	35.0	40.7	47.1	56.2	64.2	70.2	71.1	67.0	58.0	49.7	36.5
8	36.5	35.1	40.9	48.0	56.6	65.5	69.6	70.1	67.0	58.5	48.0	36.2
9	37.9	35.4	42.4	48.1	58.7	66.5	71.6	70.3	66.9	58.6	47.5	35.6
10	37.5	35.7	42.0	49.1	60.3	66.6	70.9	71.1	67.2	59.3	45.6	36.6
11	37.0	35.0	40.0	49.5	62.5	66.1	71.7	72.4	65.9	59.4	46.9	39.0
12	42.8	35.0	41.0	49.2	61.5	66.7	71.0	72.0	65.4	58.5	47.4	37.8
13	44.5	35.1	42.1	50.6	60.1	67.6	70.3	71.8	65.0	57.1	46.0	37.3
14	42.0	35.5	42.8	51.7	58.8	68.7	69.6	71.9	65.3	55.3	44.7	35.4
15	35.5	36.7	43.1	53.3	58.8	67.9	70.5	72.9	66.3	53.7	45.3	35.5
16	34.8	37.0	41.5	53.9	57.8	66.9	71.4	72.5	66.8	51.4	47.2	35.5
17	34.7	36.5	41.6	54.4	57.8	65.3	71.8	71.8	67.7	53.1	47.5	35.9
18	33.9	34.5	41.4	54.2	57.4	66.4	71.8	72.0	66.5	51.7	44.9	36.7
19	33.6	34.2	42.2	55.7	56.8	66.4	71.9	72.4	67.6	52.6	45.1	37.1
20	34.3	36.3	41.6	57.6	56.8	65.8	71.9	74.1	64.4	53.0	45.1	35.5
21	34.5	37.8	42.4	57.3	56.9	65.7	73.1	72.5	64.5	51.9	44.8	35.8
22	34.1	37.6	40.7	54.8	56.8	67.4	73.0	72.0	65.1	50.9	45.9	36.5
23	33.6	37.3	41.0	53.2	58.4	68.6	72.8	71.4	64.9	48.6	43.1	38.3
24	35.6	36.9	42.8	52.8	59.7	69.9	71.5	71.7	64.8	47.3	43.2	36.6
25	34.9	37.0	44.7	53.0	60.0	69.8	70.8	71.7	64.5	46.2	41.1	34.9
26	33.8	35.9	45.0	52.7	61.3	70.7	71.8	70.9	63.3	47.1	39.9	35.1
27	33.8	34.6	45.1	52.5	61.8	69.7	73.2	70.8	63.0	47.6	40.5	34.9
28	34.8	36.1	45.4	54.0	61.2	69.2	73.7	70.9	62.4	47.8	41.5	35.0
29	36.3	37.6	48.1	54.3	62.0	69.9	75.1	69.9	61.5	47.8	41.5	36.6
30	37.5		47.6	55.6	62.6	70.5	76.5	70.2	60.2	48.5	43.6	37.4
31	37.6		46.5		63.9		76.9	68.9		49.9		38.7
Avg F	**38.0**	**35.9**	**41.9**	**51.6**	**58.8**	**66.7**	**72.1**	**72.2**	**65.6**	**54.2**	**45.6**	**36.7**

Mount Storm Temperature:

Only available data from USGS:

Monthly mean in deg C (Calculation Period: 2001-10-01 -> 2007-09-30)												
Year	Jan	Feb	Mar	Apr	May	Jun	Jul	Aug	Sep	Oct	Nov	Dec
2001										11.0	6.1	3.9
2002	1.8	4.7	7.8	12.7	15.7	19.3	21.6	21.3	17.5	12.4	9.9	3.5
2003	1.9	4.4	8.1	11.8	15.7	19.4	21.6	23.6	20.7	12.5	12.1	5.0
2004	3.3	4.0	9.9	12.8	19.3	19.1	20.3	19.6	21.9	13.2	11.3	6.1
2005	6.5	5.0	6.1	11.8	15.7	19.0	21.7	20.4	17.4	12.0	7.0	4.8
2006	8.3	4.5	7.1	13.6	15.6	18.9	22.5	21.7	16.8	12.4	11.2	5.5
2007	6.5	1.7	8.7	10.3	17.0	19.4	19.8	21.9	17.6			
Avg C	4.7	4.1	8.0	12.2	16.5	19.2	21.3	21.4	18.6	12.3	9.6	4.8
Avg F	40.5	39.4	46.4	54.0	61.7	66.6	70.3	70.5	65.5	54.1	49.3	40.6

Detailed look I calculated using daily data between 2002 and 2006:

Mean of daily values for each day for 5 years of record												
Day	Jan	Feb	Mar	Apr	May	Jun	Jul	Aug	Sep	Oct	Nov	Dec
1	41.9	39.7	38.4	50.1	60.0	66.3	70.3	72.6	66.0	58.7	54.6	47.6
2	43.2	39.4	37.7	50.1	59.9	64.7	70.5	74.1	65.4	59.6	53.5	42.6
3	46.0	39.8	39.6	51.3	57.2	62.3	70.3	75.5	66.9	61.1	51.9	40.5
4	47.2	39.1	40.1	50.1	57.5	62.8	70.5	74.3	66.8	59.3	51.6	41.9
5	46.3	37.8	43.2	49.3	58.6	63.3	70.7	72.2	67.7	58.3	52.6	41.8
6	44.7	38.6	45.1	49.5	59.3	63.7	70.9	70.2	68.1	56.0	54.1	40.7
7	41.3	40.0	47.3	49.5	57.3	63.9	69.5	69.0	67.0	57.5	55.6	40.2
8	40.6	39.7	46.7	51.3	57.8	65.4	70.8	68.4	66.6	59.0	53.8	39.5
9	41.9	39.7	47.8	52.2	61.3	66.1	72.9	68.1	67.6	57.0	52.8	39.3
10	40.6	39.9	46.9	53.9	62.7	65.9	73.0	68.8	67.0	57.6	48.8	40.5
11	39.5	39.1	44.6	53.1	63.2	65.4	72.5	70.5	66.7	57.3	50.0	42.5
12	40.6	40.0	45.3	52.3	60.3	66.4	71.4	72.1	65.6	56.5	49.2	43.2
13	41.6	40.2	45.1	54.3	60.3	68.1	70.4	68.9	64.3	55.1	49.4	42.5
14	40.0	41.2	47.1	55.0	60.9	68.7	70.1	68.4	65.0	52.6	50.1	43.1
15	39.0	41.7	47.3	56.0	60.7	66.6	70.3	71.5	66.3	51.0	51.5	42.4
16	38.4	41.5	45.1	55.9	60.8	64.6	70.7	70.2	67.3	51.7	52.4	41.3
17	37.7	40.3	46.0	56.3	61.1	65.6	70.3	69.5	69.4	50.9	52.8	40.0
18	36.5	39.2	45.5	57.2	60.5	66.9	69.8	69.5	68.2	52.4	50.0	41.0
19	36.5	39.7	46.4	59.3	60.8	66.3	69.9	70.5	67.5	55.6	50.4	40.8
20	36.5	41.6	46.5	59.9	62.5	64.8	70.5	71.7	66.0	55.4	50.1	38.2
21	36.3	41.8	47.4	60.2	62.9	65.2	71.6	70.3	67.2	54.2	50.4	40.0
22	36.1	42.4	45.6	57.8	62.2	67.4	71.0	69.6	66.5	53.1	50.6	40.6
23	33.2	42.3	46.4	57.1	62.9	68.2	70.5	67.8	65.3	50.2	47.5	40.8
24	36.8	43.0	48.0	57.2	62.8	69.2	68.7	67.9	63.7	48.4	47.7	39.4
25	36.8	42.7	49.8	56.4	63.0	68.1	68.4	68.2	63.1	47.7	46.7	39.0
26	36.7	38.9	48.7	56.4	64.1	70.6	69.3	67.6	63.8	49.4	45.4	39.2
27	36.0	37.7	48.8	56.4	64.5	69.4	71.8	67.8	63.8	50.4	45.5	39.0
28	38.2	37.0	49.4	57.5	64.2	68.5	74.0	68.4	62.4	52.5	46.5	40.5
29	39.8	43.3	52.6	57.3	65.6	70.4	72.2	68.4	62.7	53.1	46.3	41.8
30	41.3	0.0	51.4	58.0	65.6	70.1	72.3	69.0	60.6	53.6	50.4	42.4
31	40.8	0.0	50.0	0.0	65.6	0.0	71.1	67.6	0.0	54.7	0.0	44.5
Avg F	39.7	40.3	46.1	54.7	61.5	66.5	70.8	70.0	65.8	54.5	50.4	41.2

Made in the USA
Middletown, DE
04 September 2021